I0797276

lonely planet

ART DESTINATIONS

DESTINATIONS ART

70 Places to See Great Art

CONTENTS

***Next spread:** Italy's Venice Art Biennale showcases contemporary installations by artists from 100-plus countries around the world.*

Reykjavík & beyond
Oslo
Helsinki
Glasgow
Amsterdam
Cologne
EUROPE
Berlin
London
Cornwall
Giverny
Paris
Vienna
Bratislava
Lausanne
Venice
Provence
Barcelona
Rome
Istanbul
Yerevan
Mallorca
Athens
Nicosia (Lefkosia)
ASIA
Beijing
Seoul
Tokyo
Naoshima
Marrakesh
Cairo
Kathmandu
Doha
Jeddah
Mumbai
Dakar
AFRICA & THE MIDDLE EAST
Harar
Bangkok
Manila
Penang
Singapore
Dar es Salaam
Kakadu National Park
OCEANIA
Maputo
Cape Town
Wimmera-Mallee
Melbourne
Tasmania

AMERICAS
Vancouver
Winnipeg
Detroit
Chicago
Hudson Valley
New York City
San Francisco
Santa Fe
Los Angeles
Marfa
Miami
Mexico City
Oaxaca
Antigua
AMERICAS
Lima
Brumadinho
Rapa Nui
(Easter Island)
Valparaíso
Buenos Aires
Punta del Este
Central &
orthern Islands,
Vanuatu
Nouméa
OCEANIA
Plymouth
Wellington

SWAG

Above: *Jody Paulsen's felt collages at Cape Town's Zeitz MOCAA, South Africa;* ***Opposite:*** *Andrés Reisinger's Take Over Jeddah hangs in Al Balad, Saudi Arabia.*

AFRICA & THE MIDDLE EAST

CAPE TOWN, SOUTH AFRICA

Dynamic art in the heart of the city

WHEN TO GO

Year-round.

GETTING THERE

From Cape Town International Airport (CPT), it's about 30 minutes to the city centre, home to most museums and galleries.

Art is everywhere in Cape Town – in its galleries, its world-class museums, its street murals and its public sculptures. And, the art scene's scope is all-encompassing, reflecting Cape Town's topography and geographical setting, its often tortured history and its hope-filled present.

Take in sculptures by contemporary South African artists at the **Norval Foundation**. Understand the influences shaping Irma Stern's artwork at the **Irma Stern Museum**. Journey through artistic periods and styles at the **South African National Gallery**. Relive local history in the street art of Woodstock and the townships of the Cape Flats. Take time to learn about the public sculptures you'll spot around the V&A Waterfront and the city's Foreshore area. Seek out Cape Town's many smaller (but excellent) private galleries. And, visit the groundbreaking **Zeitz Museum of Contemporary Art Africa (Zeitz MOCAA)**, where the historic silo in which it is housed is as much a part of the experience as the art exhibits themselves. Today, the most exciting developments in Cape Town's art scene are taking place at such exhibition spaces as **Youngblood Africa** and the many galleries, including **Stevenson** and the **Goodman Gallery**, working to promote new talent and forge links between local artists and their international contemporaries.

Right: *Michele Mathison's charcoal and acrylic-resin Landscapes, part of the permanent collection at Zeitz MOCAA;* ***Opposite:*** *The Zeitz MOCAA galleries are built around a reimagined grain silo at Cape Town's V&A Waterfront.*

ZEITZ MOCAA

The Zeitz Museum of Contemporary Art Africa remains one of the most ambitious and forward-looking art undertakings on the continent. Call in at the museum's atelier residency programme space, where it is sometimes possible to observe the current artist-in-residence.

YOUNGBLOOD AFRICA

Cape Town's contemporary art scene is young and dynamic, and focused on promoting new local talent. One of the best ways to gain entrée is to head to Bree St on First Thursdays, when galleries stay open until late. A highlight: Youngblood Africa, an artistic hub with workspaces and exhibits showcasing artists from Cape Town and elsewhere on the continent.

MAPUTO, MOZAMBIQUE

An independent spirit

Mozambique's artistic heritage was forged around the rallying cry of *A luta continua* – 'the struggle continues'. Dating to the country's independence war with Portugal, the sentiment it expresses continues to shape Mozambican artistic expression today.

Bold colours, fantastical figures – often intertwined – and a grandness of scale are all hallmarks of Mozambican artwork, which envelops and draws in its viewers with a unique intensity. Maputo is the hub, with the flagship **National Art Museum** and several outstanding private galleries. These include the **Fernando Couto Foundation**, which serves as a centre for literature and the arts; **Arte d'Gema**, a platform for up-and-coming artists; and the **Kulungwana** exhibit space. Maputo also has a longstanding **street-art** legacy, with an exceptional collection of dramatic murals. Mozambique's far north – currently mostly off-limits due to brutal guerrilla fighting – is the traditional home of the Makonde, who are known for their exceptional carvings, including wooden *mapiko* masks and highly detailed tree-of-life carvings. Elsewhere in the country, the arts scene finds some of its most beautiful expression in the sandalwood carvings of the far south, and intricate basketry-making traditions in the south and centre.

WHEN TO GO
Year-round.

GETTING THERE
From Maputo International Airport (MPM), it takes about 30 minutes to get to the city centre, where you'll find most major galleries.

Below: *Preparing the nets at a fishing beach in Mozambique's seafront capital, Maputo;* ***Left:*** *Bold strokes and vibrant colours are the hallmarks of Maputo's street-art scene.*

NATIONAL ART MUSEUM

The Maputo-based National Art Museum showcases Mozambique's rich and multilayered artistic traditions and features works by luminaries of the Mozambican arts scene, including Malangatana, Bertina Lopes, Roberto Chichorro, Naguib Elias Abdula and Alberto Chissano.

CASA-MUSEU DE MALANGATANA

Malangatana Valente Ngwenya (1936–2011) was a pioneer in forging a postcolonial artistic style that combines indigenous artistic traditions with international influences. Malangatana was recognised as a UNESCO Artist for Peace, and his influence continues to guide current Mozambican artists. The artist's home, on Maputo's outskirts, still contains many of his pieces. Plans are underway to convert it to a museum, but visits can be arranged with advance notice.

DAR ES SALAAM, TANZANIA

Artistic innovation and community

WHEN TO GO

Year-round.

GETTING THERE

From Dar es Salaam's international airport (DAR), it's about 40 minutes to the city centre, from where the art hotspots are within easy reach.

The congested main streets and sandy back lanes in Dar es Salaam have given rise to a lively arts scene. Start out at the small but excellent **Undarey Art Gallery**, the private exhibition space of Undarey Mtaki, one of Tanzania's most acclaimed young artists. His work is particularly notable for its geometric patterns, everyday themes and refined use of colour.

The low-key **Nafasi Art Space**, just north of the city centre, is another hub. *Nafasi* means both 'space' and 'opportunity' in Swahili, and the local arts community finds plenty of both here, sharing ideas, platforms and exhibits. Stop by the quiet compound to check out works by Tanzanian artists, both up-and-coming and established. Watch especially for pieces by **Mwandale Mwanyekwa**, one of Tanzania's most notable female Makonde sculptors. Also watch for works by pioneering Makonde artist **George Lilanga** (1934–2005). Lilanga's *shetani* carvings and paintings – depicting caricaturised evil spirits – still influence Tanzanian artists today, although you are more likely to find his originals in galleries abroad.

TINGATINGA ARTS COOPERATIVE SOCIETY

After the untimely death of self-taught artist Edward Saidi Tingatinga in 1972, his followers organised themselves into a cooperative that, with Swiss funding, continues to flourish today as a space where you can speak with artists and watch them work. The Tingatinga style is notable for its brightly coloured enamel paints and fanciful animal designs.

MWENGE CARVERS' MARKET

A small community of Makonde elders trains young artists to carry on generations-old carving traditions that originated in the forests of southern Tanzania and northern Mozambique. The carvers still travel to the Tanzania–Mozambique border to source the essential *mpingo* (African blackwood) for the most authentic pieces. Some of the carvings are on an epic scale: the largest are up to 2m (6.5ft) in height, and can take over six months to complete.

Above: *Artists use traditional techniques to make the pieces at Dar es Salaam's Mwenge Carvers' Market;* ***Opposite:*** *Chat with artists-at-work and take in the pieces on show at Tingatinga Arts Cooperative Society.*

DAKAR, SENEGAL

West Africa's dynamic contemporary-art capital

WHEN TO GO
November to May for bearable temperatures; mid-May to mid-June of even-numbered years for Dakar Biennale.

GETTING THERE
Dakar International Airport (DSS) is connected to Paris, New York and beyond.

The unofficial capital of Francophone West Africa attracts art lovers in the same way as its music scene draws fans of local stars such as Youssou N'Dour and Orchestra Baobab. You'll see traditional woodcarvings, batiks, pottery and *souwere* (under-glass painting) at the **Museum of Black Civilisations** and craft markets such as **Kermel** and **Soumbédioune**, while a lively gallery scene has put Dakar on the international art map.

Dakar Biennale (Dak'Art), Africa's longest-running contemporary art biennale, has since 1996 contributed to a cosmopolitan scene that attracts major artists, such as American portraitist Kehinde Wiley. The painter of Barack Obama set up **Black Rock Senegal**, an artist-in-residence programme that hosts cultural events, while South African-Australian artist Loman Pawlitschek turned her villa in the Mamelles area into the multifaceted **Loman Art House**. A B&B, cafe and rooftop venue share the creative space with Loman's 3D depictions of contemporary Senegal and exhibitions of local artists.

The central Plateau neighbourhood has several galleries exhibiting up-and-coming West African artists, such as

Oh Gallery and **Galerie Le Manège**, while Médina is home to workshops and studios. On UNESCO-listed **Gorée Island**, site-specific artworks commemorate the enslaved people who were shipped across the Atlantic from this tragic site.

GALERIE CÉCILE FAKHOURY

With spaces in Paris and Abidjan (in the Côte d'Ivoire), this contemporary Plateau gallery focuses on artists from across Africa and the diaspora who examine the continent's society, history and place in the world. The gallery represents artists including the late Senegalese painter Souleymane Keïta, and its temporary exhibitions feature multimedia collage, conceptual textiles, ambiguous photography and more.

MUSÉE THÉODORE MONOD

This museum, run by a cultural institute affiliated with Cheikh Anta Diop University, displays selections from its collection of some 10,000 artworks from 20-plus African countries. You'll see traditional masks, figurines, wooden statuettes, textiles, basketwork, pottery and more in the main neo-Sudanese 1930s building on Soweto Sq.

Above: *Na Chainkua Reindorf's Strange Flesh at the Galerie Cécile Fakhoury gallery in Dakar;* ***Opposite:*** *Handpainted designs grace the hulls of fishing boats at Dakar's Plage de Yoff.*

Vibrant spaces

Check out Dakar's dynamic studio hubs and artist collectives to experience the streetwise creativity of urban Africa. Start at **Espace Trames** on a Thursday evening, when DJs soundtrack spirited networking on the roof terrace overlooking Independence Sq, and multidisciplinary artists emerge from the industrial spaces below to clink cocktails. **Village des Arts** hosts a gallery and dozens of artists' studios, so you can buy raw woodcarvings, vivid scenes of contemporary Senegalese life and more – straight from their creators.

In the vibrant Médina neighbourhood (birthplace of Youssou N'Dour), check out the recycled art made from plastics and other urban detritus at **CRéAS I AM** gallery, set up to encourage local women to turn junk into furniture, fashion and artistic gold. Nearby **RAW Material Company** is a 'centre for art, knowledge and society', hosting resident artists, a curatorial academy, and thought-provoking exhibitions. Championing contemporary art and design since 1996, **Galerie Arte** is a surefire spot to pick up distinctive souvenirs, such as chunky Ghanaian polychrome figurines, delicate bronze statuettes from Ouagadougou, and playfully decorated *souwere* trays.

For a glimpse inside the working and living environment of a revered modern sculptor, visit the **Maison Ousmane Sow**, filled with expressive African figures by the late 'Senegalese Rodin'.

MARRAKESH, MOROCCO

Medieval to modern art

WHEN TO GO
Winter is prime arts season, from the Marrakesh International Film Festival (late November–December) to the 1-54 Contemporary African Art Fair in February.

GETTING THERE
Marrakesh Menara Airport (RAK) is 6.5km (4 miles) from the Djemaa El Fna. Taxi and hotel-shuttle rides take 20–60 minutes.

The heart of the ancient Medina remains the **Djemaa El Fna**, the first site to be added to UNESCO's Intangible Cultural Heritage list. Step into the cool concrete galleries of **DaDa Marrakesh** and you'll find new talents emerging from the latest **1-54 Contemporary African Art Fair**. But to discover the source of all this artistic inspiration, you'll have to leave familiar art scenes behind, and explore the medieval souqs, splendid mud-brick riads (courtyard houses) and secret gardens of Marrakesh.

Follow your nose past tempting aromas from spice merchants toward **Dar Si Said**, now creatively repurposed as the **National Museum of Weaving and Carpets** – delightful preparation for Marrakesh's legendary **Rahba Kedima** carpet souq. You'll find a shimmering wonderland of freshly restored 16th-century geometric *zellij* mosaics at **Ali Ben Youssef Medersa**. 'You who enter my door, may your highest hopes be exceeded' reads the inscription over the doorway of this Quranic learning centre – a blessing that continues to work its charms at nearby **Maison de la Photographie**, a serene riad housing a treasury of vintage silver-gelatin prints of Morocco dating back to 1870. If you prefer edible art, the **Moroccan Culinary Arts Museum** has mouthwatering exhibits, cooking classes, rooftop feasts and a gourmet shop.

MUSÉE BERBÈRE

When Algerian-born French fashion trailblazer Yves Saint Laurent visited Marrakesh in 1966, his life and career were forever changed. He bought expat painter Jacques Majorelle's Art Deco mud-brick retreat, and his partner Pierre Bergé's collection of Indigenous Moroccan Amazigh arts soon took over the cobalt-blue villa. Together they bequeathed the Jardin Majorelle with its Bergé Musée Berbère to the city that welcomed them.

MUSÉE YVES SAINT LAURENT

Nearby, the Musée Yves Saint Laurent showcases YSL's couture collections, original sketches, and film footage of runway shows. The museum also hosts splashy temporary exhibits by major artists, such as Emily Kam Kngwarray, Cy Twombly and Robert Rauschenberg.

Left: *Traditional rugs for sale in Marrakesh;* ***Above:*** *Discover emerging artists at 1-54 Contemporary African Art Fair;* ***Opposite:*** *A lace-like brick facade at the Musée Yves Saint Laurent;* ***Next spread:*** *The garden-swathed Musée Berbère at Jardin Majorelle.*

Gallery-hop from Gueliz to Sidi Ghanem

Start your own museum-worthy Moroccan art collection with a wander around the Art Deco Gueliz district.

The 1930s headquarters of a mining corporation is now a motherlode of Moroccan contemporary art: **Comptoir des Mines Galerie** hosts major gallery shows, provides studio space and organises art fairs across three sprawling storeys. Comparatively compact but impactful **Galerie Noir sur Blanc** takes Moroccan tradition into the future, embedding ancient Amazigh symbols into henna-and-oil abstract paintings with talismanic power. See Morocco beyond postcards at **Galerie Tindouf**, where acclaimed novelist Tahar Ben Jelloun captures marabouts (saints' tombs) in mesmerising colour, and self-taught painter Abdelmalek Berhiss traces the entrancing rhythms of Gnaoua music.

The Marrakesh art buzz becomes a roar in the industrial-chic district of Sidi Ghanem, where warehouses pulse with contemporary art and design studios. You'll never guess what's next at **Jajjah** arts space and tea salon – pop artist Hassan Hajjaj's limited-edition tea canisters, fundraisers showcasing Moroccan women rappers – and don't miss **MCC Gallery** for Moroccan multimedia shows blending photography and textile art into tactile truth.

CAIRO, EGYPT

Fresh wonder in the ancient city

WHEN TO GO
In February, Art Cairo has 25 galleries showing 3000 artworks at the Grand Egyptian Museum.

GETTING THERE
Cairo International Airport (CAI) is 21km (13 miles) from downtown Cairo, with travel times by taxi ranging from 30–90 minutes.

On your way to the pyramids, stop and look around. Cairo seems so massive and ancient it's hard to fathom, let alone navigate – but follow the art trails here, and you'll meet history-defining artistic communities that first took root by the Nile four and a half millennia ago.

Pharaohs may get all the glory in the new **Grand Egyptian Museum (GEM)** in suburban Giza, but Cairo keeps the arts alive with Old Cairo souqs lined with artisans' workshops, daring contemporary art galleries around Tahrir Sq, and modern-art museums and fair-trade artisan showcases inside Zamalek's Art Deco island villas.

On a single day in the city, you can be uplifted by the sublime geometry of Islamic Cairo's medieval mosques and floored by the wry truths of Basim Magdy's video dreamscapes at **Gypsum Gallery**. Join the downtown arts scene already in progress with photography workshops and events organised by **Photopia**, performances and art shows at Cairo cultural institutes organised by **Downtown Contemporary Arts Festival**, and treasure-hunting opportunities galore at the **Tam Gallery Summer Affordable Art Fair**. Pity poor King Tut – he tried to take Egypt's treasures with him, but the best parts are still right here in Cairo.

THE GREAT PYRAMID

The Great Pyramid at Giza has been inspiring awe for about 4600 years – and obsessive selfies for about 15. But to experience its legendary mystical 'pyramid power' at the source, enter from the base and clamber up the internal ramp to the king's chamber, where you can glimpse the granite sarcophagus of Pharaoh Khufu (aka Cheops in Greek).

THE NECROPOLIS AT GIZA

Khufu's pyramid is just one corner of Giza's vast ancient Egyptian necropolis, a UNESCO World Heritage Site. Nearby is the Great Sphinx and two other iconic pyramids dedicated to Khafre and Menkaure. In the shadow of Menkaure's pyramid, notice the massive stone mastaba for his daughter Khentkawes, who is shown wearing a pharaoh's beard and may have served as a king herself.

***Right:** Visitors take a tour inside the Great Pyramid of Khufu; **Above:** The Giza pyramids overlook heat-hazed Cairo; **Opposite:** Founded in 970 CE, Al Azhar Mosque is one of Cairo's many architectural highlights.*

Treasures of Old Cairo

Cairo's finest features aren't hidden inside a suburban sarcophagus, but right out in the open downtown. Stroll the sunny, serene *ziyada* (grounds) of **Ibn Tulun**, a 9th-century mosque with sublime geometric patterns that dazzle visitors and defy modern mathematics.

Wander al-Muizz St, from 10th-century stone-built Bab al-Futuh (northern gate) and past the colourful **Souq el-Khayamiyya** (Tentmakers' Bazaar) to towering 11th-century Bab Zuweila (southern gate), which held Mongolian invasions at bay while mosques, schools and souqs flourished along al-Muizz. Over 600 years, legendary **Khan al-Khalili** souqs have turned Cairene rituals of *qahwa* (Arabic coffee), shisha and good-humoured haggling into art forms. Nobel Prize–winning author Naguib Mahfouz credits coffee-shop gossip along Midaq Alley for inspiring his novel by that name.

Whether you choose to buy work in Old Cairo souqs or at **Fair Trade Egypt**'s showcase of 43 women-run artisan cooperatives, supporting Cairo's arts scene is increasingly vital. As part of President's Sisi's plan to build a new suburban capital, Old Cairo arts centres (along with swaths of Cairo's UNESCO-protected City of the Dead) have been bulldozed for highways. Meanwhile, behind Tahrir Sq, you may spot political graffiti art along Mohammed Mahmud St – Cairene spirits remain irrepressible, as you'll see at nearby **Cairopolitan**. Here emerging Egyptian artists show their silkscreened posters, original comics and Egyptian pop-art objects.

قهوة الفيشاوي
Silver and rosary
قهوة الفيشاوي
EL FESHAWI

MUSEUMS

Grand Egyptian Museum (GEM)
Acres of ancient Egyptian artefacts, including King Tutankhamun's 5400 treasures

Coptic Museum
Papyrus scrolls, Fayum portraits and medieval Madonnas showcase Egypt's Coptic-Christian heritage

Museum of Islamic Art
Dazzling displays cover Islamic tiles, geometric woodwork, and astonishingly accurate astrolabes

National Museum of Egyptian Civilization
Astounding Egyptian highlights, from silver-canopied camel caravans to a 3000-year-old prosthetic toe

Mohamed Mahmoud Khalil Museum
Newly reopened palace showcasing the ex-Prime Minister's 300-plus Impressionist collection

Museum of Modern Egyptian Art
Modernists line Cairo Opera House, from 1940s feminist painter Inji Aflatoun to contemporary expressionist Samir Fouad

Gayer-Anderson Museum
Ottoman mansion turned Mideast treasure-box – and James Bond movie backdrop

GALLERIES

Gypsum Gallery
Art-star launchpad, from Basim Magdy's video dreamscapes to Marianne Fahmy's dark-magic carpets

Mashrabia Gallery
Risk-taking shows by Egyptian women artists and Cairo's top emerging artists

Access Art Space
Essential contemporary arts platform revives the fearless programming of Cairo's ex-Townhouse Gallery

Art Talks
Insightful shows of accomplished Egyptian artists, from cartoonist George Bahgory to epic storyteller Ali Said

Above: *Rameses II presides over the soaring atrium of the Grand Egyptian Museum;* ***Right:*** *Exquisite tiling in the Persian Room of the Gayer-Anderson Museum;* ***Opposite:*** *A stately entrance for Cairo's Coptic Museum.*

HARAR, ETHIOPIA

The art of welcome

WHEN TO GO
Market days on Fridays and Saturdays.

GETTING THERE
Harar is 518km (322 miles) from Addis Ababa – about 10 hours via Selam Bus Line. Otherwise, travel by air or train from Addis to Dire Dawa, 53km (33 miles) from Harar.

Home to Africa's earliest Muslim communities, Harar is also one of the world's most artistically inclined, forward-thinking cities. Inside the medieval stone walls of the old city and UNESCO World Heritage site of **Harar Jugol** are 82 mosques and 102 saints' shrines. Most of these structures are ingeniously built from mud-brick and *näçih afär* (limestone mixture) to weather changing climates, painted in bright, pop-art colours.

At a Harari cultural guesthouse you'll be ushered through the courtyard of a traditional *gey gar* (city home) into a true curatorial wonder: an adobe *gidīr gār* (salon) lined with *ṭāqēts*, niches purpose-built to showcase Harari embellished basketry, glossy red-and-black earthenware, and enamelled platters for generously shared feasts. But the centrepiece here is the *ēqäd ṭāqēts*, the double niche containing such prized books as the Quran and the Bible – plus poetry in five local languages, printed by Harari bookbinders since the 16th century.

Join wide-ranging discussions fuelled by Harari coffee, and you'll see Harar as visiting dignitaries have for 500-plus years: a vibrant, interfaith, multicultural city that earns its global spotlight – and its UNESCO Cities for Peace Prize.

GREAT FIVE GATES OF HARAR

Welcoming peaceful visitors by design since the 16th century, the Great Five Gates of Harar are flanked by lively markets selling elaborate Harari baskets, utensils ingeniously crafted from recycled materials, and tailored garments created in minutes on curbside sewing machines.

TOMB OF EMIR NUR IBN MUJAHID & BATI DEL WAMBARA

Near Erer Gate is a striking green sculptural form that looks like an adobe beehive, but is actually the tomb of Emir Nur ibn Mujahid and Bati del Wambara, his wife and chief strategist, who are credited with commissioning Harar's fortified gates – and ushering in a golden age.

Above: *The emerald-painted tomb of Emir Nur ibn Mujahid and Bati del Wambara;* ***Opposite:*** *Purpose-built niches showcase traditional ceramics and basketry at a Harari cultural guesthouse.*

JEDDAH, SAUDI ARABIA

Saudi's capital of creativity

WHEN TO GO

The cooler months between December and March are ideal for exploring outdoor art installations.

GETTING THERE

Jeddah's King Abdulaziz International Airport (JED) receives direct flights from around the world, including London, Paris, New York and multiple cities across India, the Middle East and Africa.

If the uber-conservative Kingdom of Saudi Arabia has a 'rebel child', Jeddah would be it. The view of this port city – nicknamed the 'Bride of the Red Sea' – has always been out to the world, whether it's welcoming seafaring traders of yore or modern-day Muslim pilgrims journeying to the nearby holy cities of Mecca and Medina. This global gaze has long provided fodder for fresh ideas, making Jeddah a core of creative energy like no other Saudi city.

Art is embedded into the very fabric of Jeddah. Its roadsides and roundabouts contain wacky, larger-than-life displays, such as *Accident! (Crazy Speed)* – in which five full-size cars look like they've crashed head first into a giant block of concrete – and *The Four Lanterns*, modelled after lamps commissioned for Cairo's mosques by medieval Mamluk sultans, both by Spanish artist Julio Lafuente. The Corniche, the city's seaside promenade, is home to the **Jeddah Sculpture Museum**, which is actually a small outdoor park with pieces by Henry Moore, Joan Miró, César Baldaccini and others, including Saudi sculptors. The contemporary art scene in Jeddah continues to pop up in unexpected places, and it's even breathing new life into abandoned buildings in the city's historic district.

Below: *Beautifully lit by night, Julio Lafuente's towering Four Lanterns echo mosque lamps commissioned by medieval Mamluk sultans;* ***Left:*** *Hayy Jameel, arts centre and creative hub for Jeddah and wider Saudi Arabia.*

HAYY JAMEEL

'Hayy' means 'neighbourhood' in Arabic, so perhaps it's no surprise that this arts centre, opened in 2021, feels hidden away in a residential area. The futuristic space hosts cultural events of all sorts, from art exhibitions and workshops to film screenings in its 200-seat movie theatre, the first independent cinema in Saudi Arabia (such establishments were banned for nearly four decades here, until 2018).

ATHR GALLERY

Athr elevates work by Saudi and Arab creatives at prominent international art fairs, as well as across the region and at home in its Jeddah gallery on the top floor of a shopping centre. Exhibits rotate a handful of times each year.

Art in Al Balad

One of the most fascinating neighbourhoods in the Middle East is Al Balad, Jeddah's historic district. Crumbling centuries-old buildings constructed of Red Sea coral line the narrow streets, their windows covered with brightly painted teak *roshan* (wooden lattice screens), designed so that the women of the house could look outside without being seen. Originally settled in the 7th century CE, this neighbourhood was once the heart of Jeddah, but families started moving out in the 1960s as the city expanded and grew more prosperous, leaving the old buildings at the mercy of the elements.

Today, Al Balad is catching the interest of a new generation seeking to bring the neglected buildings back from the brink. Launched in 2023, **Balad Al-Fann** (meaning 'town of art' in Arabic) is a three-month-long arts festival that sees contemporary installations, large and small, take over the neighbourhood. The festival has renovated a dozen of the district's historic buildings to serve as temporary gallery spaces, showing work by Saudi, Arab and international artists. Al Balad itself is also a canvas and an inspiration, as students from the **Royal Institute of Traditional Arts** show off projects that aim to preserve the district's architecture and keep age-old ways of working alive.

DOHA, QATAR

Art and architecture in an Islamic context

WHEN TO GO

The winter period from November to February is the most pleasant season to explore Qatar's desert installations.

GETTING THERE

Hamad International Airport (DOH) is globally well-connected by flag carrier Qatar Airways and numerous international airlines.

Starting with the 2008 opening of the **Museum of Islamic Art (MIA)** in Doha, Qatar has grown into a hub showcasing Middle Eastern and North African artists as a result of heavy government investment into cultural properties across the country. This ranges from featuring locally inspired architectural forms at the **National Museum** – known for its 'desert rose' design, which emulates a rare sand crystal – to highlighting local and regional artists at **Mathaf: Arab Museum of Modern Art**.

Public art installations across the country – primarily centred on Doha but spread across 56 sites throughout Qatar – invite viewers to explore the desert landscape via contemporary sculpture and other artworks. Many celebrate Qatari traditions such as falconry and pearl-diving, as well as maritime themes. Even the 2022 World Cup stadiums were designed with an eye towards local culture to resemble forms from Qatari art and design, such as dhow sailing-ship sails, Bedouin nomad tents and *gahfiya* men's headwear.

Cultural development is a central focus for the government-run **Qatar Foundation**, maintaining a uniquely Qatari and Middle Eastern identity even while engaging with the wider-world art community, and Doha's art scene exemplifies this ethos.

Right: *Olafur Eliasson's Shadows Travelling on the Sea of the Day;* ***Opposite:*** *IM Pei's Museum of Islamic Art on the Doha waterfront;* ***Next spread:*** *French architect Jean Nouvel designed the multilayered home of Doha's National Museum of Qatar.*

MUSEUM OF ISLAMIC ART (MIA)

An architectural work of art itself, the IM Pei–designed Museum of Islamic Art incorporates traditional Islamic motifs into a modern museum design showcasing 18 galleries of artwork and artefacts from across 1400 years of Islamic history. Illustrated Qurans and ornate astrolabes are presented alongside Central Asian carpets, Andalusian sculpture and more in a tightly curated collection.

SHADOWS TRAVELLING ON THE SEA OF THE DAY

This site-specific installation by Olafur Eliasson near northern Qatar's historic Al Zubara fort envelops the viewer in desert sands as they explore 20 mirrored circular shelters held aloft by steel rings, arranged in a symmetrical pattern inspired by Islamic geometrical design forms.

İSTANBUL, TÜRKIYE

Türkiye's rich cultural palimpsest

WHEN TO GO
April, May, September or October for mild spring or autumn weather and cultural festivals.

GETTING THERE
İstanbul Airport (IST) is a major international hub, while Sabiha Gökçen International Airport (SAW) receives budget flights from Europe.

Sprawling across seven hills above the Bosphorus, the strait dividing the European and Asian continents, İstanbul has a restive creativity that embodies East and West, old and new, and many more binaries besides. In a megacity where calls to prayer wail above bars and fashion boutiques, you can admire glorious Ottoman carpets in the **Museum of Turkish and Islamic Arts**, pick up your own kilim and some tulip-decorated İznik tiles in the **Grand Bazaar**, and search **Beyoğlu** side streets for distinctive jewellery and homeware by contemporary designers.

Artwork of the ages pops from every corner – from portraits of Ottoman sultans and pashas in the magnificent **Topkapı Palace** to the street art of **Kadıköy** on the city's Anatolian shore, and from the 6th-century **Basilica Cistern**'s Medusa the Gorgon column bases to contemporary installations in the reimagined **Silahtarağa Power Plant**. To get a feel for the Ottomans who ruled İstanbul from 1453 until the decadent era of 19th-century Dolmabahçe Palace, explore Dolmabahçe's **National Palaces Painting Museum**, the nearby **Palace Collections Museum**, and the **Pera Museum**. The latter is a gem for its Kütahya tiles and Turkish Orientalist paintings, including harem scenes, courtiers' portraits, mosque-studded cityscapes, and Osman Hamdi Bey's beloved *The Tortoise Trainer* (1906).

İSTANBUL MODERN

Part of Karaköy's waterfront Galataport development, this glittering contemporary Renzo Piano–designed building houses Türkiye's first modern and contemporary art museum. The permanent collection and temporary exhibitions focus on Turkish artists, with international big-hitters such as Tracey Emin, Olafur Eliasson and Richard Wentworth also displayed across 10,498 sq metres (113,000 sq ft).

MUSEUM OF INNOCENCE

Orhan Pamuk, the Nobel Prize–winning author of *Snow* and *My Name is Red*, based this whimsical art project in Çukurcuma on his novel of the same name. The installation fills a 19th-century wooden house with artefacts relating to the book's star-crossed lovers, Kemal and Füsun, and to late-20th-century İstanbul.

Right: *Displays at Orhan Pamuk's Museum of Innocence;* ***Above:*** *Renzo Piano's sleek design echoes the collection at the İstanbul Modern;* ***Opposite:*** *The ornate Imperial Hall within the harem at Topkapı Palace.*

Religious art

The Ottoman and Byzantine empires that collectively ruled İstanbul for more than 1500 years left a rich trove of artistry in their mosques and churches. Built in the 530s for Emperor Justinian, the greatest Byzantine building, the **Hagia Sophia (Aya Sofya)** basilica, contains some of the finest treasures in its glittering mosaics of Christian and historical figures. Beneath the famous 'floating' dome, climb to the upstairs gallery and pass the runic 'street art' carved into a balustrade by marauding Vikings to find the golden mosaics, including one of Constantine the Great and Justinian offering the city and the Hagia Sophia to the Virgin Mary.

The church-turned-mosque-turned-museum was reconsecrated as a mosque in 2020, and some of the figurative mosaics are covered. The Late Byzantine **Kariye Mosque** has followed a similar trajectory; visit outside prayer times to see its gloriously restored frescoes and mosaics. İstanbul's monumental Ottoman mosques, such as **Süleymaniye Mosque** by the great imperial architect Mimar Sinan, match the Byzantines' ambition in expressing the sultans' greatness and religious devotion. The Hagia Sophia's neighbouring **Sultanahmet (Blue) Mosque** typifies the fine artisanship of these minaret-flanked landmarks. Beneath its cascade of 17th-century domes, more than 20,000 floral İznik tiles and 250 stained-glass windows bathe the vast prayer space in its renowned blue glow.

High Hazard
Medium Hazard
Low Hazard
Dangerous Marine Life
15 ST

***Above:** Susan Point's People Amongst the People in Vancouver's Stanley Park, Canada;*
***Opposite:** South Beach lifeguard hut, Miami, USA.*

AMERICAS

WINNIPEG, CANADA

Home of the world's largest Inuit art collection

WHEN TO GO
Winnipeg is liveliest June through September.

GETTING THERE
You can fly to Winnipeg International Airport (YWG) from across Canada and from US cities, including Atlanta, Chicago, Denver, Las Vegas, Los Angeles and Minneapolis.

Though this prairie city in central Canada may not be on as many art-focused travellers' radars as cultural hubs like New York or Paris, Winnipeg is nonetheless home to the world's largest museum devoted to Inuit art. A 3716-sq-metre (40,000-sq-ft) exhibition centre at the **Winnipeg Art Gallery (WAG)**, **Qaumajuq** opened in 2021. It houses more than 25,000 Inuit art pieces, many drawn from the WAG's own collection assembled since the 1950s, along with works on loan from the government of Nunavut, the territory that's home to more than half of the Inuit population in Canada.

Winnipeg has a many-generations-long Indigenous heritage, as the traditional territory of the Anishinaabe (Ojibwe), Ininew (Cree) and Dakota peoples, and of the Red River Métis, whose lineage combines Indigenous and European roots. Where the Red and Assiniboine Rivers meet, the Forks is now a National Historic Site as well as a popular food hall, and has been an Indigenous meeting place for centuries.

Francophone culture thrives in Winnipeg's St Boniface district, while the annual August Folklorama fest celebrates

the city's diversity. Also in Winnipeg is the Canadian Museum for Human Rights, the world's first museum dedicated to human rights in its many forms.

QAUMAJUQ

Located in downtown Winnipeg and led by an Indigenous curatorial team, this luminous Inuit art museum features a dramatic three-storey glass vault displaying thousands of carvings, as well as changing exhibits of sculpture, textiles, prints, drawings and digital media. Qaumajuq's goal is to 'bring the North to the South', showcasing Inuit art and culture in a region that's easier for many to reach than the Inuit homelands.

WINNIPEG ART GALLERY

Qaumajuq's parent organisation, the Winnipeg Art Gallery has a permanent collection that primarily encompasses works by Canadian and European artists. First opened in 1912, the WAG's exhibits draw from its own collections and from travelling art shows.

Above: *Michael Maltzan's white-stone and glass building houses the 25,000-strong Inuit art collection at Qaumajuq;* ***Opposite:*** *Spring Celebration, by Roger Aksadjuak and Laurent Aksadjuak, at the Winnipeg Art Gallery.*

VANCOUVER, CANADA

Where Indigenous art thrives

WHEN TO GO
April through October (July and August are busiest). Winter brings rain and chilly temperatures but also more cultural events.

GETTING THERE
Vancouver International Airport (YVR) is a 25-minute SkyTrain (metro) ride from downtown. Amtrak trains run from Seattle, Washington, and Portland, Oregon.

Vancouver sits pretty on the Pacific Coast, a city of glass and steel that towers between the mountains and the sea. Yet beneath this modern exterior, the largest metropolis in western Canada has deep Indigenous roots, with evidence of settlement in the region dating back more than 10,000 years – centuries before the first European settlers arrived.

Vancouver's art scene reflects this Indigenous influence – beginning at the international airport, which has a celebrated collection of Indigenous art that greets arriving visitors. Totem poles and welcome figures stand in **Stanley Park**, the vast urban rainforest that borders the city's downtown. The park – and greater Vancouver – are located on the traditional territory of the Coast Salish First Nations, including the Musqueam, Squamish and Tsleil-Waututh peoples. Indigenous-owned Talaysay Tours offers guided walks in Stanley Park that highlight First Nations' history and culture.

MUSEUM OF ANTHROPOLOGY

On the University of British Columbia campus west of the city centre, this modern museum houses one of the world's top collections of Northwest Coast Indigenous art and artefacts. Totem poles, canoes and other carvings line the colossal Great Hall; another highlight is *The Raven and the First Men*, an immense cedar sculpture by Haida artist Bill Reid.

BILL REID GALLERY OF NORTHWEST COAST ART

Showcasing the life and works of one of the region's most noted First Nations artists, Bill Reid (1920–98), this downtown Vancouver gallery also exhibits art by other Indigenous artists from around the region.

Left: *Ellen Neel's Kakaso'Las, Museum of Anthropology;* ***Above:*** *Indigenous Northwest Coast art and artefacts in the Museum of Anthropology Great Hall;* ***Opposite:*** *Bill Reid's The Raven and the First Men, at the Museum of Anthropology.*

Indigenous art today

Indigenous art in Vancouver is a vibrant, evolving practice, with artists from many of the 203 First Nations in British Columbia living and working in the city.

You'll find works by Musqueam artist **Susan Point** throughout the region, including *Cedar Connection*, a treelike cedar sculpture at Vancouver International Airport; her red-cedar welcome portals, *People Amongst the People*, are installed in Stanley Park.

Another Musqueam artist, **Debra Sparrow**, is known for her weaving, and has been blanketing the city – literally. In a multiyear project dubbed *Blanketing the City*, Sparrow has created massive murals inspired by patterns found in Coast Salish weaving. Look for these works on Granville Island and in downtown's Cathedral Sq.

You can also see designs by contemporary Indigenous artists in Canada's first Indigenous art hotel. Inside **Skwachàys Lodge**, a boutique lodging in Vancouver's Gastown neighbourhood, each of the 18 guest rooms features one-of-a-kind designs by First Nations artists.

Coastal Peoples Gallery in Gastown shows works by Northwest Coast First Nations and Inuit artists. **Douglas Reynolds Gallery** on South Granville St specialises in contemporary Northwest Coast art, exhibiting museum-quality pieces by artists such as Robert Davidson, of Haida and Tlingit heritage, and the late Kwakwaka'wakw master carver Beau Dick.

HUDSON VALLEY, USA

A river runs through it

WHEN TO GO

Fall foliage (October–November) is unforgettable.

GETTING THERE

Dia Beacon is 1km (0.6 miles) uphill from Beacon Station on Metro North's Hudson line (combo museum-train ticket available). Olano is 5km (3 miles) south of Amtrak's Hudson train station.

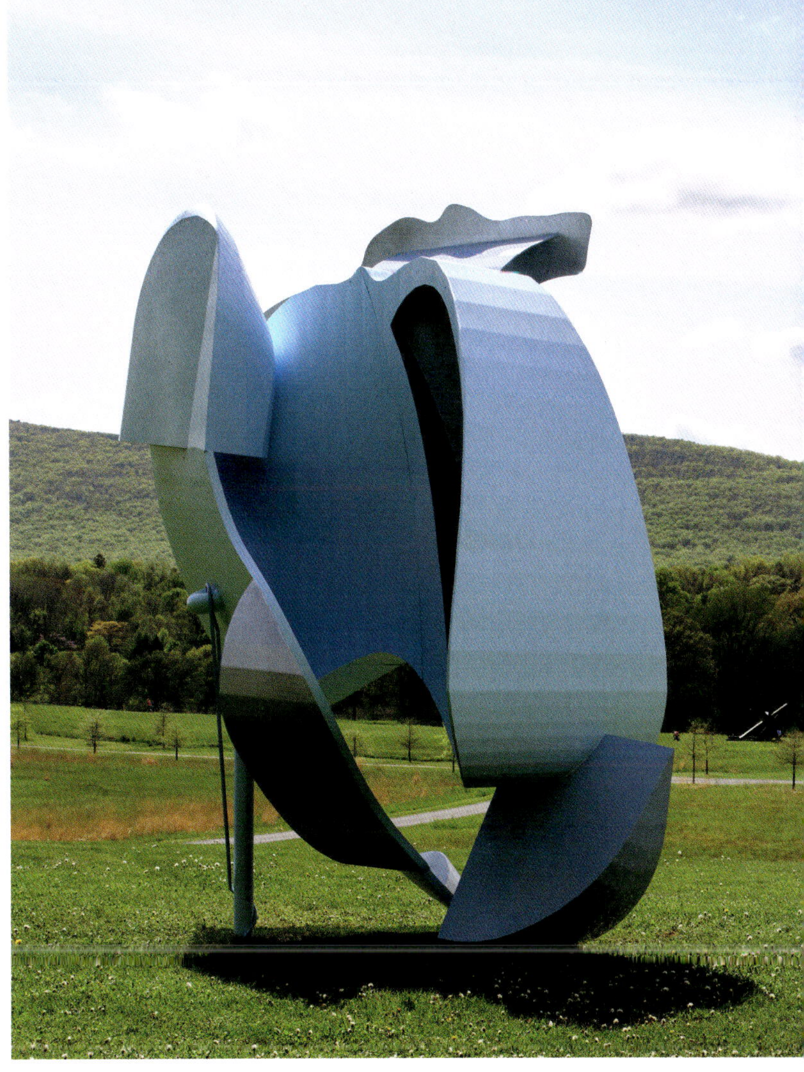

Steaming on a passenger train alongside this sinewy ribbon of slate-blue, wending its way from New York Harbor north, passing abandoned island castles and Rip Van Winkle bridges, on tracks cleaved from multicoloured granite and bordered by forest, it's easy for travellers to imagine the inspiration felt by artists from the notable **Hudson River School** – Frederic Church, Thomas Cole and others – to the present.

From the sheer cliffs of the Palisades to the Catskills of Church's inspiration, it's still possible to envision the region as these important artists saw it a century ago. Indeed, Hudson Line trains have run on these same tracks since the mid-19th century. **Storm King Art Center**'s undulating 202 hectares (500 acres) in Cornwall are an outdoor art lover's dream; and one can get inside the mind (and studios) of Church and Cole at their homesteads further upriver. In fact, for the sturdy of foot and lung, there is a 6.4km (4-mile) River Skywalk connecting the two artists' properties just outside Hudson.

DIA BEACON

Dia Beacon was born from the real deal: a defunct Nabisco box-printing plant turned museum. Warhol's *Shadows* has a room here, as do other post-'60s luminaries. Seasonally changing gardens compete with rotating shows indoors. A side trip to outdoor sculptures of Storm King, just across the bridge, is worthwhile.

OLANA

Frederic Church found his spiritual and artistic centre on this hilltop eyrie. Just miles from his mentor Thomas Cole's property (follow the Hudson River Skywalk across the river to reach the Thomas Cole National Historic Landmark, the farm/studio of the Hudson River School's 'founding father'), Church envisioned Olana's 101 hectares (250 acres) of orchards, gardens and pathways – now a state park open to the public – as a work of landscape art.

Above: *Bea Blue by Arlene Shechet, one of more than 100 artworks scattered across the Hudson Valley grounds of Storm King;* ***Opposite:*** *Frederic Church's wildflower-wreathed former home on his Olana estate.*

USA

Everywhere's art in New York City

NEW YORK CITY,

WHEN TO GO

April, May, September and October usually deliver the most temperate weather, without summer or holiday crowds.

GETTING THERE

As a major international travel hub, NYC is easily reachable by car, bus, boat and major airlines.

New York City is one of the world's greatest art scenes. Artists seeking Bohemian fellowship were first drawn here in the 19th century, but it was abstract expressionism – America's first homegrown artistic movement to gain real international influence – that made NYC the epicentre of the art world in the mid-20th century. Today, NYC's art museums are some of the greatest in the world. Keep an eye out for their special free and reduced-admission days.

NYC is also a major centre of the international art market. It is home to auction houses, art fairs and hundreds of commercial galleries, especially in Manhattan and Brooklyn. Manhattan's Chelsea is arguably the most notable arts district, full of free-to-visit, white-walled galleries, including the **Gagosian**, **Hauser & Wirth**, **David Zwirner** and **Marianne Boesky**. A gallery crawl is best on Thursday or Friday night, when openings are common.

Also in Chelsea is the **High Line**, an elevated rail line repurposed as a public park; it's packed with art and surrounded by incredible architecture. Nearby SoHo claims the **Judd Foundation**, the living and working space of Donald Judd and one of NYC's few visitable artists'-home museums.

Right: *David Cooper's Brooklyn Chic mural in the street-art hotspot of Bushwick;* ***Opposite:*** *The elevated High Line weaves in between apartment buildings and includes unexpected places to sit, surprising art, and stunning views.*

METROPOLITAN MUSEUM OF ART

The Met (including its uptown annexe, the Cloisters) is the fourth-largest and second-most-visited art museum in the world. Masterwork and magnum opus upon chef-d'oeuvre and priceless treasure swell the galleries behind its sweeping beaux-arts facade. Even those boasts don't capture its grandeur – a head-spinning display of 5000 years of art from across the globe.

BUSHWICK COLLECTIVE

Notable and amateur taggers have used local Bushwick businesses' walls as canvases for 50-plus commissioned murals along Brooklyn's St Nicholas Ave and adjacent streets. There are other spray-painted nexus in NYC, but none as concentrated, copious or captivating, or as splashy a confirmation of graffiti as art.

Museum of Arts and Design (MAD)

Now in its third incarnation since being founded in 1956 (and located at 2 Columbus Circle since 2008), MAD is as much a celebration of artistic process as an exhibition of creative output. Its provocative and participatory programming dives into the ideas, influences, environments, materials and impacts of artistic and utilitarian objects.

Importantly, MAD also brings artists themselves to the public. On the top floor of its six levels, working creatives occupy three artist studios, at least one of which is usually open during museum operating hours on certain days. (There is also a hands-on learning space with impressive views of Columbus Circle.) Visitors are encouraged to step into an active studio and engage directly with the artist or designer, a unique museum privilege. Competition is fierce for these six-month residencies, and it shows in the high-calibre work – and makers – on display.

MAD's exhibition and interaction area is modest in size. The premium on space means displays are carefully curated, favouring interdisciplinary collections and engagements that purposefully blur the lines between art, craft and design, and embrace all artisans accomplished in their work. Visitor experience associates lead worthwhile guided tours (free with admission), including the artist studios.

4:35 PM

seth
globepainter
SUNBELT
972418
2669RT

DETROIT, USA

Comeback city with art at its heart

WHEN TO GO

April through November, although most venues are open all year.

GETTING THERE

Cabs, Metro Cars and Detroit Air Express from Detroit Metro Airport (DTW) to downtown. Public transport is minimal; best to rent a car or Uber.

When Detroit hit rock bottom, abandoned factories that once rolled out four-wheeled Detroit muscle became must-sees for tourists eager to experience a modern-day archaeological excavation of a storied city buried in its own decay. But Detroiters staged one of the greatest comebacks of all time, with its resident art community widely contributing to the city's revival – from large-scale street murals to visionary galleries hosting a diverse range of artistic voices. Anchored by the world-class collection at the **Detroit Institute of Arts**, the city features 30–40 weekly art exhibitions of local talent.

The city continues to rehab architectural gems from its early-20th-century heyday, and Detroit's exceptional design history was confirmed when it was named as America's first City of Design by UNESCO in 2015. Structures such as the Art Deco **Guardian Building**, with its striking tangerine-brick exterior, blend Native American, Aztec and Arts and Crafts design influences. Legendary architect Albert Kahn designed the **Fisher Building** with a three-storey arcade adorned with frescoes, mosaics, marble and brass.

The art and design community supported Detroit when it was down – and now, as the city restores its pioneering sparkle, the creative scene is exploding amid this new-found commitment to its creative roots.

LIBRARY STREET COLLECTIVE

JJ and Anthony Curis are the force behind Library Street Collective, exhibiting artists like Shepard Fairey and undertaking a neighbourhood-wide revitalisation project in the East Village – including an outdoor public installation of the late Charles McGee's sculptures, which welcome visitors to the Shepherd, a 110-year-old Romanesque church transformed into a cultural arts centre.

CRANBROOK ACADEMY OF ART

The Eero Saarinen influence at Cranbrook Academy of Art is evident in its architecture, and as the original academic model proved so successful, it remains largely undisturbed. The grounds – including its museum and gardens – are open to the public, and you can tour Frank Lloyd Wright's Smith House.

Right: *Charles McGee Legacy Park at the Library Street Collective's Shepherd Arts Center;* ***Above:*** *The art-adorned Belt, a Detroit alleyway revitalised by the Library Street Collective;* ***Opposite:*** *The Mothership Connection by Zak Ové at the Shepherd.*

Michigan Central Station

Detroit's ill-famed abandoned buildings are becoming scarce as the city rises from its ash. Of particular note is the newly renovated Michigan Central Station. No longer the premier example of 'ruin porn', emblematic of a city's deterioration, it has become the jewel in Detroit's revitalisation and a symbol of its renewed future.

The spectacular beaux-arts-style building was designed by Warren & Wetmore and Reed & Stem, the same architects who worked on New York's Grand Central Station. Painstaking efforts were made to restore every original embellishment, including the Guastavino ceiling tiles and marble floors. While the building now gleams, some of the graffiti that covered the previously decaying walls has been preserved as a reminder of that chapter in the station's history. An open archive, portrait gallery and reading room invite visitors to explore artefacts and unexpected treasures.

Ford Motor Company's investment in this historical building as a technological hub has also engaged Detroit's art and cultural community through public art installations and performances. The station sits in a 12-hectare (30-acre) walkable campus, located in Corktown, and in addition to arts programming also hosts restaurants – such as Slows Bar BQ and Honey Bee Market, where the house-made chorizo is a local favourite.

The Frank Lloyd Wright Trust

America's most famous architect opened his first practice in Chicago in 1893, and quickly made a name for himself. The city was still recovering from the Great Fire of 1871, which levelled more than 17,000 structures, so new building was sorely needed. His Prairie Style – so-called because it was designed to fit in to the flat Midwestern landscape – marked a turn towards creating a uniquely American architecture. He went on to design some of the county's most iconic buildings, from the balanced-over-a-waterfall Fallingwater to New York's spiral-shaped Guggenheim Museum. But Chicago is the city he left the biggest effect on, and today, lovers of design and architecture can tour several Wright properties.

The Frank Lloyd Wright Trust runs tours of Wright's home and studio in **Oak Park**, where a self-guided walking tour takes visitors past several other Wright-designed properties. Also in Oak Park is **Unity Temple**, a Unitarian Universalist church that's the only surviving public property from the Prairie period. In Hyde Park, the elegant **Robie House** is open to tours as well. Downtown, the **Rookery** is an early high-rise office building with an ornate Wright-designed lobby, all white Carrara marble and Persian arabesque patterns.

MARFA, USA

Small city, big art

WHEN TO GO
March through May: temperatures are cool, wildflowers are in bloom.

GETTING THERE
Marfa is 97km (60 miles) south of Interstate 10. The closest commercial airports are in Midland (MAF) and El Paso (ELP), both some 306km (190 miles) away.

There is something elusive about Marfa, with its remote location in the Big Bend region of far West Texas: an empty high desert where the crisp, clear air feels like a separate presence. This stark landscape appealed to Donald Judd, an artist and art critic who moved to Marfa from New York City in 1971. Here he would create permanent art installations that used the desert and an abandoned army base as a canvas for his three-dimensional sculptures. These striking minimalist works put Marfa on the art-world map. Today, Marfa is a cattle town with strong artistic bona fides and good food. Anchored by a classic town square and courthouse, downtown Marfa hosts a compelling mix of locals – artists, cattle ranchers and Border Patrol agents – who easily coexist. Galleries and boutiques hug a grid of streets where the design-minded Hotel St George doubles as a downtown hub. The **Judd Foundation** offers tours of Judd's home and studios. And every visitor leaves downtown at some point to scan the horizon for the mysterious Marfa Lights. According to lore, these mystery lights occasionally flicker below the dark Chinati Mountains. Look for them from the viewing area on Hwy 90 east of town.

Below: Approaching Marfa from West El Paso Street;
Left: Art installation turned tourist attraction:
Elmgreen & Dragset's Prada Marfa.

CHINATI FOUNDATION

The artillery sheds at the Chinati Foundation hold a captivating encapsulation of Judd's minimalist vision. Guided tours are required to view the sheds and the rest of the permanent collection, which includes a fluorescent light installation by Dan Flavin and an outdoor sculpture by Claes Oldenburg and Coosje van Bruggen.

PRADA MARFA

This glossy duplicate of a Prada store was commissioned by the Art Production Fund and Ballroom Marfa. Its creators, Elmgreen & Dragset, hoped to trigger thoughts about the meaning of high fashion when viewed outside an urban setting. The Texas Department of Transportation classified the structure as a museum in 2014.

SANTA FE, USA

High art in the high desert

WHEN TO GO

Collectors plan around Santa Fe's summertime trio of art markets: Folk Art, Hispanic and Native Treasures.

GETTING THERE

Albuquerque International Airport (ABQ), aka Sunport, is about 105km (65 miles) from Santa Fe.

Wander the Santa Fe Trail and you'll slip through time portals to an artistically inspired past, present and future. For millennia this high-desert crossroads has been home to Ancestral Puebloan peoples, who left deep imprints on nearby **Petroglyph National Monument** and designed the iconic adobe architecture that defines modern Santa Fe. Today, visionary Indigenous futurism movements launch at the Institute of American Indian Arts' **Museum of Contemporary Native Arts (MoCNA)**.

Each new arrival brings fresh tales and starry-eyed desert visions to the Southwest's 400-year-old trading post – and centuries of cultural exchange continue to inspire artistic breakthroughs at galleries downtown, along **Canyon Rd**, and in the **Railyard District**. Witness the meteoric rise of art stars at **SITE SANTA FE**, or join kids tumbling through refrigerator doors into an immersive multiverse at **Meow Wolf** – the Chief Worldbuilder here is *Game of Thrones* author George RR Martin.

RAILYARD DISTRICT

Follow your bliss into the Railyard District, home to excellent year-round farmers and art markets, several of the city's best galleries, and contemporary arts launchpad SITE SANTA FE. This free-form staging ground for immersive art shows is entirely transformed by visiting international curators and the world's most exciting artists – including Venice Biennale star Jeffrey Gibson and his rainbow-beaded LGBTIQ+ guardian figures.

MUSEUM OF CONTEMPORARY NATIVE ARTS (MoCNA)

For a clear view to the future without losing sight of the past, head downtown to the Museum of Contemporary Native Arts. This avant-garde gallery is backed by the illustrious Institute of American Indian Arts, the fine-arts college founded by and for Native American artists in 1962.

Left: *Indigenous fashion at Santa Fe's Museum of Contemporary Native Arts;* ***Above:*** *Ancestral Puebloan rock art, Petroglyph National Monument;* ***Opposite:*** *Meow Wolf's House of Eternal Return.*

Making a Life
Creando una Vida
Gallery
Galeria
9

See through Georgia O'Keeffe's eyes

On Santa Fe's Lowrider Day, you might spot a Georgia O'Keeffe–inspired, skull-airbrushed art car parked outside the **Georgia O'Keeffe Museum** – and indoors, the paint still looks just as fresh on her skull-strewn local landscapes. Painter Georgia O'Keeffe's iconic skyscrapers and sensuous flowers were the talk of New York when she escaped to New Mexico in 1929. Luminous desert sunlight, sun-bleached skulls and hieroglyphic clouds opened new possibilities for her – and the rest is art history, as you'll see in her landmark museum. The museum also offers guided tours of her adobe home-studio in **Abiquiú**, 97km (60 miles) north of Santa Fe, where old bones and modern sculpture dot the house and garden. Road-trip onward to her summertime getaway, **Ghost Ranch**, and you'll see just how brilliantly she evoked these dramatic, striped canyon vistas. Make advance preparation for when inspiration might strike by picking up art supplies and attending hands-on painting workshops at Santa Fe's **Ecole des Beaux Arts**, or visual storytelling labs at **Center for Advancing the Photographic Arts**. Postcards are nice, but as Georgia O'Keeffe knew, there's no better souvenir from Santa Fe than the one you create.

GALLERIES

Smoke the Moon
Moving, meticulous works in breakthrough shows by emerging artists

Chiaroscuro
Transfixing contemporary shows balance light and dark, meditative and provocative

Owings Gallery
A century of Southwestern masterworks, from Agnes Pelton's surrealism to Tony Abeyta's prismatic landscapes

Nüart Gallery
Graphic textiles and collages that look like mystical signage for spiritual traffic

Hecho a Mano
Contemporary Southwestern artists meet historic Mexican masters

Zane Bennett/form & concept
Two sister galleries under one Railyard District roof. Zane Bennett promises conceptual showstoppers, from Jaune Quick-to-See-Smith's alternate-history scenes to Priscilla Dobler Dzul's handwoven, life-size Volkswagen; while art, craft and storytelling converge at the genre-bending form & concept gallery

Left: *Jenny Day installations at Zane Bennett form & concept gallery;* ***Above:*** *Adobe style at the New Mexico Museum of Art;* ***Opposite:*** *Nancy Friedland show at Santa Fe's Smoke the Moon gallery.*

MUSEUMS

Museum of International Folk Art
Imaginations race through 150 nations, finding common ground in miniature ceramic villages and spent-bullet flower gardens

New Mexico Museum of Art
Landmark adobe shows local pride, from 1930s murals to TC Cannon's Native pop-art portraits

Museum of Indian Arts & Culture
Native curators celebrate living legacies, from modern Diné textiles to sci-fi Pueblo ceramics

Vladem Contemporary
NMMA's extension showcases massive new works, including Leo Villareal's light installations

Wheelwright Museum of the American Indian
Deep collections and standout shows, including blown-glass totems by Tony Jojola

SAN FRANCISCO, USA

Bohemian art by the bay

WHEN TO GO

Spring brings the San Francisco Art Fair.

GETTING THERE

San Francisco Airport (SFO) is 18km (11 miles) south of the city. BART (Bay Area Rapid Transit) trains get you to/from the airport to downtown SF in 20–30 minutes.

San Francisco is home to three world-class art landmarks known for adventurous collections – **SFMOMA**, **de Young**, **Legion of Honor** – as well as museums that celebrate SF's diverse global roots and boundless imagination, including the **Asian Art Museum**, **Contemporary Jewish Museum** and **Museum of the African Diaspora**. Underground art is loud and proud in SF, with psychedelic '60s rock posters lining the legendary **Fillmore Auditorium** and freshly silkscreened skate graphics and protest posters at **Haight Street Art Center**.

The experimental ethos that inspired hippies, Beat poets and Burning Man tinkerers continues to spark rainbow raves, public poetry and totally trippy technology. Self-driving cars and splashy noncommercial art converge in SF's waterfront Dogpatch district, where the art and tech are often odd, but not necessarily at odds. Big-tech angel investors back radical poster art at **Letterform Archive**; nonprofit **Institute of Contemporary Art San Francisco (ICASF)** hosts immersive video art and food-art pop-ups; and **Minnesota Street Project** stages breakthrough gallery shows of emerging artists. Keep an eye on SF's waterfront, where the world's biggest light-art installation is going even bigger: **Bay Bridge Lights** will be switched back on in 2025, after crowdfunding raised US$11 million to illuminate the entire span from SF to Oakland.

SFMOMA (SAN FRANCISCO MUSEUM OF MODERN ART)

Take on SFMOMA's sprawling collection of 33,000-plus artworks from the top: wallow in immersive soundscapes, navigate Olafur Eliasson's *One-Way Colour Tunnel*, and take a breather in minimalist Agnes Martin's hexagon room. Then take in the showstopping photography – one of the world's first and finest museum collections of photographic arts.

DE YOUNG MUSEUM

Curators here boldly pursue ideas across cultures and art forms, so you never know what awaits around the corner – don't miss Ruth Asawa's mesmerising woven-wire pods casting alien shadows on gallery walls, James Turrell's *Skyspace* hidden under the sculpture garden, and panoramic park vistas atop the 44m-high (144ft) observation tower.

Above: *The tectonic crack of Andy Goldsworthy's Drawn Stone runs across de Young Museum's Diller Court;* ***Opposite:*** *SFMOMA's collection is displayed in a purpose-built space designed by Norwegian architects Snøhetta.*

San Francisco's artistic alleys

Art fans don't just flock to SF to see familiar favourites – they look here to see what's next. The extended 1930s SF honeymoon of Frida Kahlo and Diego Rivera kicked off the city's century-long love affair with massive multicultural murals, inspiring 1934 **Coit Tower** murals showing San Francisco life during the Depression. Since the 1970s, Mission *muralistas* have captured pride and protest in the district's 700-plus murals, from historic Latina-led **Balmy Alley** pieces maintained by nonprofit Precita Eyes to the collectively run **Clarion Alley Mural Project**, a skate-punk-inspired collective that launched the Mission School movement in the 1990s with artists Rigo, Megan Wilson and Barry McGee. Serving SF since 1979, the **Women's Building** was covered in glory by seven women Mission *muralistas* and 100 volunteers with the five-storey *MaestraPeace*, showing goddesses and feminist icons working wonders – on the Lapidge St side, you'll spot Nobel Prize-winner Rigoberta Menchú overhead and artist Georgia O'Keeffe hanging out on the corner. Around the corner at **500 Capp St**, the Mission District home of late conceptual sculptor David Ireland now serves as an arts nonprofit and environmental artwork, filled with experimental art installations – be part of the ongoing social sculpture with free self-guided Saturday visits.

SILENCIO=MUERTE
MORE FUNDS FOR ♀s
HEALTH RESEARCH
6 Ft
Stay 6 feet apart

UNCONVENTIONAL MUSEUMS

Exploratorium
Stop time, sculpt fog and more, with hands-on experimental exhibits

Cartoon Art Museum
Iconic comics, from Batman to Trina Robbins' underground feminist comics

Museum of Craft & Design
Handcrafted originals celebrate humanity in AI-obsessed SF

Legion of Honor
Contemporary art winks at classics, from John Cage soundscapes to Monet water lilies

Institute of Illegal Images
'The Blotter Barn' features 40 years of LSD-infused postage-stamp art

Above: *Interactive exhibits at the Exploratorium;*
Middle: *Turn the page on counterculture at City Lights;*
Opposite: *A 'room composition' waiting to happen at Audium.*

GENRE-DEFYING PERFORMANCES

Oasis
Only-in-SF drag, from drunk Disney singalongs to NSFW PowerPoints

City Lights
Readings are revelations at the Beat bookstore and free-speech landmark

SFJAZZ
Inspired improvisation, featuring jazz legends, poets – and skateboarders on percussion

Audium
Listen to the floor: Audium blends found sounds into trippy 'room compositions'

SF Mime Troupe
Tony Award–winning musical satires make crowds laugh, sing and sign petitions in SF parks

LOS ANGELES, USA

City of angels and art movements

WHEN TO GO
Sunny SoCal makes LA a year-round destination, but expect larger crowds in the summer.

GETTING THERE
Fly to Los Angeles International (LAX) or Hollywood Burbank (BUR) airports, and take the LA Metro to major landmarks. Rent a car or rideshare to visit local neighbourhoods.

With a star-studded history dating back to the 1920s beginnings of Hollywood's Golden Age, Los Angeles is a popular destination for film lovers and pop-culture fans worldwide. The LA art scene also sprang up during the 20th century, with the arrival of collectors and curators and the founding of museums and galleries. The renowned **Chouinard Art Institute** opened in 1921, its graduates going on to work in film and carve out their place in conceptual art movements. Other art schools such as **ArtCenter** and **CalArts** soon followed, contributing to LA making its name as a hub for fine artists, designers, filmmakers and animators. Artists and social activists in Los Angeles also empowered and advocated for their communities through storytelling, performance and grassroots arts movements.

Today, art aficionados can view famous works by both Old Masters and modern artists alike in museums like **LACMA**, the **Getty**, the **Huntington** and the **Norton Simon Museum**. For an extra memorable experience, be sure to spend time at more specialised collections – such as at the **Academy Museum**, **Hammer Museum** and the **Corita Art Center** – to trace LA's fascinating history not only as a global arts and entertainment capital, but also as a city that embodies multiculturalism and creative community organising.

Below: *The gardens surrounding hilltop Getty Center;* ***Left:*** *Historical and contemporary art inside the Hammer Museum, at UCLA.*

GETTY CENTER

Located on the hills overlooking LA, the Getty is home to a world-class museum, research library and conservation institute. Visitors take a tram ride to access the campus' bright architecture, scenic gardens and wide-ranging art collections. Check out Van Gogh's *Irises*; rooms of paintings, sculpture and decorative arts; and rotating displays (including photography) in the West Pavilion.

LOS ANGELES COUNTY MUSEUM OF ART (LACMA)

The biggest museum of art in the western US, LACMA houses a collection of over 150,000 works, including pieces by Picasso, Magritte and Diego Rivera. Don't forget to commemorate your visit with photos alongside *Urban Light* by Chris Burden, the iconic public-art installation of historic street lamps at the front of the museum.

Where arts thrive in community

The greater Los Angeles area spans multiple neighbourhoods, making LA's artistic landscape as diverse as its communities. Beyond major museums, consider visiting local establishments and organisations that have served as birthplaces of impactful art movements.

LA's jazz scene came to life in South Central from the 1930s to the '50s, when greats like Billie Holiday, Duke Ellington and Ella Fitzgerald frequented clubs on Central Ave, and the **Dunbar Hotel** became a gathering place for Black performers in a segregated Los Angeles. Today, South LA remains a home for African American artists and musicians. Closer to downtown, in the Little Tokyo Historic District, learn important history at the **Japanese American National Museum**, enjoy delicious snacks at local eateries, visit fun shops and see a performance from **East West Players**, the country's first professional Asian American theatre company. Further inland, the Chicano Mural Movement flourished in East Los Angeles during the 1970s and '80s, with public art that embraced cultural pride splashing the walls of schools, churches and city buildings. Today, organisations like **Self Help Graphics & Art** continue celebrating Chicana/o and Latinx art. Literary arts also thrived across LA's diverse neighbourhoods through the work of the Venice Beat and Leimert Park poets, Watts Writers Workshop and the Eastside Chicano poets; the queer and punk scenes also contributed to the city's ongoing spoken word movement.

MUSEUMS & GALLERIES

The Huntington
Scholarly research institution with a picturesque library, art museum and botanical gardens

Norton Simon Museum
Mid-sized museum with works by Rembrandt, Degas, Picasso and others.

Getty Villa
Immersive recreation of an ancient house, filled with Greek and Roman antiquities

Museum of Contemporary Art (MOCA)
Contemporary paintings, installations and media art at two buildings in downtown LA

The Broad
Contemporary art by Basquiat, Koons, Kruger, Kusama, Lichtenstein, Murakami and more

Hammer Museum
Unique exhibits and programmes, including the Made in L.A. biennial

Academy Museum of Motion Pictures
Exhibits and programmes dedicated to the history, science and the art of cinema

GRAMMY Museum
Interactive exhibits on music making, featuring Grammy award-winners

Autry Museum of the American West
Art and artefacts documenting the West, including large Native American art collections

Japanese American National Museum
Powerful exhibits and programmes on Japanese American history and culture

California African American Museum (CAAM)
Exhibits and programmes preserving African American history, art and culture

LA Plaza de Cultura y Artes
Museum and community centre celebrating Mexican American and Latinx culture

Craft Contemporary
Exhibits featuring contemporary artists influenced by craft and folk art

Hauser & Wirth
International art gallery with locations in downtown LA and West Hollywood

Gallery Nucleus
Work by illustrators, cartoonists, graphic artists and pop-culture storytellers

ARCHITECTURAL & CULTURAL LANDMARKS

Watts Towers
National Historical Landmark of massive steel sculptures adorned with mosaics and found objects

Walt Disney Concert Hall
Stunning steel structure designed by Frank Gehry and home to the LA Philharmonic

Hollywood Bowl
Historic amphitheatre and current-day live music and performance venue

Griffith Observatory
Astronomy museum and planetarium; LA's most-visited public observatory

Los Angeles Central Library
Public library with an Art Deco exterior and historic decorative arts within

Dunbar Hotel
Historic cultural landmark; gathering place for Black artists during LA's Jazz Age

Stahl House
Iconic mid-century modernist house designed by Pierre Koenig

Hollyhock House
Highly stylised residence designed by Frank Lloyd Wright; a UNESCO World Heritage Site.

Corita Art Center
Organisation preserving the work of pop artist, educator and activist Corita Kent

Self Help Graphics & Art
Community art centre known for printmaking workshops, exhibits and outreach programmes

New Beverly Cinema
Historic movie theatre showing classic films and cult favourites

Bob Baker Marionette Theater
LA historic-cultural monument, still presenting fun, family-friendly puppet shows today

Judson Studios
Architectural and stained-glass studio operating for over 125 years

Clockwise from top left: *The dynamically designed Broad Museum; The planetarium dome at Griffith Observatory; The Frank Gehry–designed Walt Disney Concert Hall; Gothic-style spires atop the mosaic-adorned Watts Towers.*

FREE GENERAL
ADMISSION

LA PHIL STORE

MEXICO CITY, MEXICO

Where art prevails

WHEN TO GO

CDMX Art Week in February for Latin America's largest art fair: ZonaMaco.

GETTING THERE

Benito Juárez International Airport (MEX) is about 5km (3 miles) from downtown Mexico City. Near Terminal 1 is Terminal Aérea Station; hop on Metro Line 5 downtown.

To see what Mexico City holds closest to its heart, head into the **Centro (**historic centre) along Paseo de la Reforma, Mexico City's grandest avenue. Here Indigenous artist-activists deposed a French Christopher Columbus statue in 2020 to install **Glorieta de las Mujeres que Luchan** (Roundabout of the Women Who Fight). The modified monument commemorates resistance to gender violence with a defiant sculpture dubbed *Justicia* (Justice), flanked by the names of missing or murdered Indigenous women. Keep your eyes open for performance art in progress on downtown streets – you never know when sculptor Chavis Mármol might crush another Tesla with a 8165kg (18,000lb) stone replica of an Olmec head.

Around Alameda Central Park, explore the restless inventiveness and curative colour schemes of **Museo de Arte Popular**; the defiant dark humour of Posada's laughing-skeleton woodblock prints at **Museo Nacional de la Estampa**; and the joyous cultural pride of Ballet Folklórico performances at mural-swagged, Maya-inspired Art Deco **Palacio de Bellas Artes**. Follow the current of crowds to nearby **Zócalo**, where an entire Aztec pyramid has recently emerged after centuries hidden in the shadows of the cathedral and presidential palace. In Mexico City, politics may change, but the art endures.

Right: *A beautifully brutalist building houses the contemporary collection of Museo Rufino Tamayo;* ***Opposite:*** *Interior artworks at the Museo de Arte Popular, a major showcase for Mexican folk art.*

MUSEO NACIONAL DE ANTROPOLOGÍA

Time-travel through 3000 years of Mexico's finest moments at Museo Nacional de Antropología. Here you can pay respects to Mexico's original icons: Tenochtitlan's Sun Stone Aztec calendar; pre-Hispanic ceramic figurines of Mexico's beloved hairless Xolo dogs; and the intimidating 2000-year-old jade mask of Zapotec bat god Murcielago – miraculously recovered after Mexico's most notorious art heist.

MUSEO RUFINO TAMAYO

Steps away from Mexico's ancient wonders is modernist Museo Rufino Tamayo, featuring mural masterworks by the museum's namesake. Contemporary shows here are quietly provocative, from Adriana Varejão's scenes of colonial unrest emerging from blue-tiled *azulejos* walls to conceptual sculptor Tania Pérez Córdova's melted and painstakingly reconstructed buckets, pots and other domestic supplies.

Frida, Diego & friends

For landmark art with a side of wild romance, follow the footsteps of Frida Kahlo and Diego Rivera around Mexico City. Start at Kahlo's birthplace and home-studio, **Casa Azul**, where she created soul-searching surrealist self-portraits after a debilitating trolley-car accident. She met her husband Diego Rivera at Mexico City's **Ministry of Education**, where he was working on his own masterpiece: 33 murals celebrating the importance of education to defend the rights and freedom of women, Indigenous people, workers, scientists and artists.

In the Ministry's *Ballad of the Revolution* mural, Rivera depicts Kahlo as a radical heroine – a role she played in real life when she extended asylum at Casa Azul to Leon Trotsky and his wife Natalia Sedova, revolutionaries escaping a death sentence meted out by Stalin. Kahlo and Rivera relocated to ingeniously conjoined home-studios, now open to the public in San Angel as **Museo Casa Estudio Diego Rivera y Frida Kahlo**. Two years later another nearby safe house was found for the dissidents, but Stalinist assassins tracked down and killed Trotsky at this hideaway, now preserved for posterity as **Museo Casa Leon Trotsky**.

After Frida's death in 1954, Diego turned Casa Azul into a museum in her honour. It would be Diego's last great work: he died a year before it opened in 1958.

HOUSE MUSEUMS

Casa Museo Leonora Carrington
Dreams come alive at the great surrealist's creatively chaotic apartment

Museo del Objeto del Objeto
Showcasing CDMX pop-culture obsessions, from gig posters to soccer gear

Casa Gilardi
Minimalist Luis Barragán's house is an immersive colour-theory masterclass

Museo Casa Leon Trotsky
Witness the meticulously recreated assassination scene and radical art gallery

Museo Dolores Olmedo
Spanish-era hacienda filled with pre-Hispanic and anticolonial Rivera artworks

MEGA MUSEUMS

MUAC (Museo Universitario Arte Contemporáneo)
World-class glass jewel-box museum showcasing Mexican modernists plus international provocateurs

Museo Anahuacalli
Pre-Hispanic and modernist masterpieces fill Rivera's mosaic-studded, Teotihuacán-inspired 'Temple of the Arts'

Museo Jumex
Sprawling installations and heart-pounding performances rock this Veracruz travertine monolith

Museo Soumaya
Witness Carlos Slim's purchasing power: Rodins, sundry surrealists, and Diego Rivera's final mural

Castillo de Chapultepec
Mexico's 50-year revolution echoes through Siqueiros and Tamayo murals in the ex-imperial palace

Above: *Colour meets minimalism at Luis Barragán's Casa Gilardi;* ***Right:*** *The sinuous aluminium-tiled shell of Museo Soumaya;* ***Opposite:*** *Sunlight streams through stained-glass windows at Castillo de Chapultepec.*

OAXACA, MEXICO

Every art form, every day

WHEN TO GO
Oaxaca's spirits are celebrated not just on Día de Muertos (1–2 November), but through most of October.

GETTING THERE
Xoxocotlán Airport (OAX) is about 13km (8 miles) from downtown Oaxaca, or 20 minutes by taxi or shuttle bus.

No matter what medium you pursue, all creative roads eventually lead to Oaxaca. Follow trailblazing Mexican photographers from the 1920s to today from **Centro Fotográfico Manuel Álvarez Bravo** to **Centro de las Artes de San Agustín**, an 1883 textile factory an hour outside the city, now ingeniously repurposed as a stunning contemporary photography and art centre. **Museo Textil de Oaxaca** celebrates local artisans and global outlooks, featuring Zapotec weavers inspired by Mahatma Gandhi and feminist statements stitched into Panamanian *mola* applique. If you're a collector, don't miss the gift shop here and the nearby government-run **ARIPO Craft Center**, known for *alebrijes* – Oaxacan woodcarvings of fantastical creatures.

In Oaxaca, you'll even find art in the post office: **Museo de Filatelia de Oaxaca** hosts themed exhibits of stamp art from Mexico and around the world, plus a deep archive of stamps to explore by country and topic. To see more works on paper or even print your own, visit **Instituto de Artes Gráficas de Oaxaca** – a living legacy of legendary Zapotec graphic artist Francisco Toledo – and browse the graphic-arts studios lining Calle Porfirio Díaz.

TEMPLO DE SANTO DOMINGO

The 16th-century Templo de Santo Domingo remains active today, with murmured prayers indoors and raucous *callejoneadas* (wedding processions) led by *mojiangas* (giant puppets) on the doorstep. The cloisters have been thoughtfully converted into a Oaxacan cultural centre, featuring Zapotec relics, a stunning library with illuminated manuscripts, and rare pre-Hispanic plant life in the ethno-botanical garden.

MUSEO RUFINO TAMAYO

This treasury of pre-Hispanic art is where ongoing ethnographic research reveals the backstories of ancient local Mixtec and Zapotec artefacts, tracing connections to Maya, Olmec and Aztec civilisations – as well as the 16 distinct, diverse Indigenous communities with homelands in modern Oaxaca state.

Above: *Wedding celebrations in front of Oaxaca's Templo de Santo Domingo;* ***Opposite:*** *Woodcarver at work in the artisan village of San Martín Tilcajete, just outside of Oaxaca.*

ANTIGUA, GUATEMALA

Craft capital of the Americas

WHEN TO GO

Antigua has a pleasant spring-like temperature all year round. The dry season runs November–April.

GETTING THERE

Antigua lies about 40km (25 miles) west of Guatemala City Airport (GUA). The drive can take up to 90 minutes in traffic.

Antigua was the capital of Guatemala for more than 200 years. When Guatemala City replaced it in the 18th century, it morphed into a living museum of the Spanish colonial era. Those historic facades now lead to trendy coffee shops, boutique hotels and museums of both modern and pre-Columbian art. Yet the real reason many come to this UNESCO World Heritage Site is to shop for museum-quality arts and crafts – mostly from the Maya communities living in the surrounding highlands.

Antigua has more handicraft shops per capita than anywhere else in Central America, making it a regional hub for both traditional goods and modern variations. At concept stores such as **Luna Zorro**, **Wakami** and **Colibri** you'll find pine-scented raffia baskets, folksy ceramics, colourful wooden festival masks and beaded jewellery. Maya have woven and dyed fabrics for more than 2000 years, so the intricate textiles (now crafted on treadle looms) are Antigua's biggest collector's items. Complex geometric patterns once found only on traditional clothing have been adapted to table runners, pillowcases and handbags. You'll also see woven wall-hangings and carpets that, while inspired by the past, are imbued with a more contemporary look.

MUSEO NACIONAL DE ARTE DE GUATEMALA (MUNAG)

The National Museum of Guatemalan Art opened in stages between 2021 and 2022 within a 16th-century royal palace on Antigua's main square. Those historic walls now come alive with hundreds of artworks spanning more than 3000 years, from the pre-Columbian era up to both the colonial and Republican periods. Some of the oldest pieces hail from Maya archeological sites such as Tikal.

LA NUEVA FÁBRICA

This nonprofit contemporary art space lies next to an artisanal textile factory on a 16th-century church plaza. Its curators encourage interdisciplinary collaboration between international artists and local art communities, staging temporary exhibits to complement the permanent collection from the late Guatemalan photographer Lissie Habie.

Above: *Brightly painted festival masks for sale in Antigua;* ***Opposite:*** *Artisan weavers display traditional Maya textiles outside the town's Iglesia el Carmen.*

LIMA, PERU

Where Incan artefacts meet modern art

WHEN TO GO
Lima is mostly dry and cloudy; you'll have a better chance of sunshine December–April.

GETTING THERE
Lima's Jorge Chavez International Airport (LIM) – 11km (7 miles) northwest of the city – is well-connected to Europe and the rest of the Americas.

The Peruvian capital has a bit of everything for art lovers. There are labyrinthine museums – like the **Museo de la Nación** and the **Museo de Oro** (Gold Museum) – with wowing collections of pre-Columbian art. The former lies within an archaeological site, Pachacámac, which is one of several ancient ruins that dot the city (others, like the adobe pyramid of Huaca Pucllana, are right in the heart of downtown Lima). Then, there are the grandiose Spanish colonial-era collections at **Museo Pedro de Osma**, or the more modern exhibits at the **Museo de Arte Contemporaneo**. Photography fans flock to the **Museo Mario Testino**, which is dedicated to its namesake Peruvian fashion photographer, who has captured everyone from Taylor Swift to Diana, Princess of Wales.

Lima is also home to vibrant street art splattered across the walls of its more bohemian sectors, including the colourful **Barranco** neighbourhood, the city's creative core. Here, you'll find a dozen or so galleries and even art-themed hotels, including Hotel B, which is blanketed in hundreds of paintings, prints and photographs. Another enclave with a superb contemporary art scene is upmarket **San Isidro**, with fashionable galleries and its own art hotel, the six-room Atemporal.

MUSEO LARCO

The thousands of pre-Columbian ceramic vessels displayed within this gorgeous museum – including the world's largest collection of erotic pottery – would be enough to make it a showstopper. But there is also intricately woven textiles, quixotic masks and lavish headdresses, not to mention entire rooms dedicated to works in silver and gold.

DÉDALO ARTE Y ARTESANÍA

Take a tour of the finest Peruvian handicrafts from the Amazon to the Andes at this labyrinthine store in the Barranco neighbourhood. There are entire rooms dedicated to alpaca textiles, silver jewellery, vibrant festival masks and anthropomorphic pottery. Plus, you can dine at Dédalo's serene patio café.

***Right:** Pre-Columbian ceramic figures in the Museo Larco; **Above:** Street art in the Barranco barrio, Lima's creative core; **Opposite:** Lima from above, lapped by Pacific Ocean waves.*

The culinary arts

Should food be considered art? The answer is an unequivocal *yes* at the fine-dining establishments of Lima. The city's most vaunted gastronomic temples consistently rank toward the top of prestigious lists such as the World's 50 Best Restaurants. In fact, Lima's most famous restaurant, **Central**, was ranked No 1 on that list in 2023. Chef Virgilio Martínez crafts a culinary journey across Peru from the Andes to the Amazon, serving plates that appear on your table like edible modern art.

No less attractive are the dishes on the *dégustation* menu at nearby **Maido**, where chef Mitsuharu Tsumura explores the Nikkei, or Japanese-Peruvian fusion food, that gave this nation many of its most renowned plates. That includes the modern style of ceviche, as well as its cousin, *tiradito*, which Tsumura typically presents in a painterly fashion (imagine thin strips of raw fish floating in vibrant yellow and orange sauces).

Elsewhere in town, you find Venezuelan-Peruvian fusion foods at **Mérito**, hearty Creole cuisine at **Isolina** and sustainable seafood from the Pacific coast at **El Mercado**. At each of these famed restaurants, the quality of the food is as important as the aesthetics on the plate, making dining in Lima a showcase of ephemeral art.

BRAZIL

The marvel that is Inhotim

BRUMADINHO,

WHEN TO GO

Dry season (between April and September) for less rain and cooler temperatures.

GETTING THERE

Many one-day visitors come from the nearby state capital of Belo Horizonte, 60km (37 miles) north. Belvitur Transfer and Cia Coordenadas Bus Lines offer transfer and bus services.

Latin America's largest open-air art gallery, the **Inhotim Institute** is spread out over 140 hectares (346 acres) of rolling fields and palm forests in Brumadinho, a historic mining town in the Brazilian state of Minas Gerais. A series of botanical gardens and lakes create a symbiotic relationship between the surrounding nature and the galleries and pavilions that showcase the work of dozens of international artists such as Chris Burden, and Brazilian artists like Adriana Verejão.

Founded by the controversial Brazilian billionaire Bernardo Paz, Inhotim's collection has only grown larger over the years, with plenty of room for expansion. Museumgoers need at least a full day, if not two or three, to explore the whole complex and take in everything from audio installations such as Janet Cardiff's **Forty Part Motet**, a room where 40 speakers mimic the effect of being surrounded by a choir; and John Ahearn and Rigoberto Torres' **Abre a Porta** (Open the Door) and **Rodoviária de Brumadinho** (Bus Station of Brumadinho). The latter piece, dedicated to the community of Brumadinho, is particularly resonant following the catastrophic dam collapse that the town suffered in 2019.

Right: *The view through Olafur Eliasson's kaleidoscopic Viewing Machine;* ***Opposite:*** *Inhotim installations include Hélio Oiticica's Invention of Color, Penetrable Magic Square #5, De Luxe;* ***Next spread:*** *The 'kinetic carpet' of Yayoi Kusama's Narcissus Garden.*

NARCISSUS GARDEN

Yayoi Kusama's *Narcissus Garden*, a 2009 installation, is a kinetic artwork comprised of 750 steel balls floating in a shallow reflecting pool, moving and shifting with the wind. The artist premiered the original version of this piece at the Venice Biennale in 1966.

GALERIA ADRIANA VAREJÃO

Brutalism is in its full glory in this gallery that, from the outside, looks like a floating box of concrete – but as you step inside, a more complex structure is revealed. Works on show include Varejão's *Celacanto Provoca Maremoto* (Coelacanth Provokes Seaquake), inspired by traditional Portuguese titles.

BUENOS AIRES, ARGENTINA

Cultural capital of South America

WHEN TO GO
September to November and March to May offer pleasant temperatures and fewer crowds. Come in December and February for the warmest temps.

GETTING THERE
Fly to Buenos Aires' Ministro Pistarini International Airport (EZE), or take a bus from Argentina's neighbouring countries.

To many, Buenos Aires is the intellectual and arts capital of all South America. BA moves with the formality of a European city, while also retaining the rhythms, history, sensibilities and energy of its Latino roots. Art, tango, passion and poetry take to the streets in the storybook neighbourhoods of **Palermo**, **Recoleta** and **San Telmo**. As one of Argentina's most famed writers, Jorge Luis Borges, once said: 'Without the streets nor dusks of Buenos Aires, a tango cannot be written.'

With a vibrant local arts scene, the city attracts big-name talents from across the world for art festivals like **ArteBA**, gallery showings, and rotating exhibits at the city's world-class museums. Buenos Aires' gilded past comes to light in the intriguing collections dedicated to Eva Perón, Bartolomé Mitre and small-time eccentrics such as Xul Solar, who had a love affair with floating cities and winged mythical creatures. Better yet, most museums are free to the public.

For performing arts, don't miss a tour and show at the world class **Teatro Colón**; its stage has been graced by Enrico Caruso, Maria Callas, Luciano Pavarotti and 'Weird Al' Yankovic, to name a few.

MUSEO DE ARTE LATINOAMERICANO DE BUENOS AIRES (MALBA)

This is perhaps one of the finest collections of Latino art in the world. Wonder at the masterworks of Diego Rivera, Frida Kahlo, Fernando Botero, Antonio Berni and Tarsila do Amaral, along with rotating exhibits that attract the freshest talents from across the western hemisphere.

MUSEO NACIONAL DE BELLAS ARTES

At the Museo de Bellas Artes in the tony Recoleta neighbourhood, you will find South America's largest collection of European art, with inspiring canvases by Goya, Van Gogh, Monet, Titian and others. The remarkable collection of Argentinean art features paintings, lithographs, sculptures and photographs from some of the nation's most famous artists.

Left: *Taking in Antonio Berni's The Great Temptation or The Great Illusion at MALBA;* ***Above:*** *Museo Nacional de Bellas Artes;* ***Opposite:*** *Tango alfresco in Buenos Aires' Belgrano district.*

VALPARAÍSO, CHILE

Art, clouds, poetry and passion

WHEN TO GO
Spring and summer (October–April) are best.

GETTING THERE
Valparaíso is just 116km (72 miles) from Santiago. You can get here by bus or car. Day-trippers could consider a guided tour from Santiago, but an overnight is worth it.

Art and poetry come alive in the hard-fought port city of Valparaíso, Chile. It's grimy, it's gritty, it's wonderfully run down. And somehow it all works in a symphony of colours, street art, lost stairways that run into the clouds, and mighty funiculars that pull locals and tourists alike to the top of the city's hills. Established as a UNESCO World Heritage Site, Valparaíso's **architecture** is something to behold. The signature corrugated tin roofs and industrial-age seaport buildings are punctuated by proud-standing cathedral towers that rise up above the din of the port town. It's a steampunk dream with a uniquely Latin American twist.

As you climb through the city's amazing labyrinth of stairways and alleys, you can marvel at what could be Latin America's finest collection of **street art**. Each year, artists continue to add to this living canvas, which now includes well over 1400 unique pieces. Stop for a moment for a refreshing pisco sour at an open-air cafe to connect with the vibe and spirit of this city that was born from the poetic heart. No wonder Chile's poet laureate, Pablo Neruda, drew so much inspiration from this 'nonsense...crazy, insane port.'

LA SEBASTIANA

Hike up through the Bellavista neighbourhood to the holiday home of Chile's most beloved poet, Pablo Neruda. Known as La Sebastiana, the towering four-storey building includes a whimsical collection of art and other curios collected by Neruda and friends over the years.

PARQUE CULTURAL DE VALPARAÍSO

Tens of thousands of people were detained, tortured or disappeared in Chile during the Pinochet dictatorship. To create a new spirit of art and cooperation, the city's former prison complex has been converted into a premiere arts venue. Today, the Parque Cultural de Valparaíso offers gardens as well as rotating art exhibits, round-tables, performing arts, music, theatre and dance.

Above: *Inside the Parque Cultural de Valparaíso, where former prison blocks now host a vibrant arts centre;* ***Opposite:*** *La Sebastiana, former home of Pablo Neruda and now open as a museum.*

CHILE

Ancient art in the South Pacific

RAPA NUI (EASTER ISLAND),

WHEN TO GO

The ocean is warmest from November to May. Rates spike in the high season between January and March.

GETTING THERE

Rapa Nui is only accessible via Santiago, Chile. There are daily direct flights with LATAM Airlines.

How could a society cut off from the rest of the world grow so prolific that it left behind nearly 1000 monumental stone heads? That is the mystery of Rapa Nui (Easter Island), a remote Chilean territory in the South Pacific, which is blanketed in the artistic legacy of the ancient Rapa Nui people. Their monolithic human figures, known as **moai**, rise to an average height of 4m (13ft), can weigh as much as 12,700kg (2800lb), and were likely hewn between the 12th and 17th centuries.

The running theory among archaeologists is that the Rapa Nui 'walked' their moai to stone platforms in an upright position, using ropes. Less than 20% actually made it to the revered ceremonial sites, known as *ahu*, which are located mostly along the coast. In fact, nearly 400 moai remain as works-in-progress at the main quarry and workshop, the volcanic crater of **Rano Raraku**. Nearby is the largest *ahu*, **Tongariki**. Its 15 moai stare inland, their backs to the ocean. Remarkably, none of the moai stood vertical on their *ahu* at the end of the inter-clan warfare that rocked the island in the 18th and 19th centuries. Those upright today have been meticulously restored.

MUSEO RAPA NUI

This small but vital museum is the only place on the island to see the rare Rongorongo tablets, which are covered in symbols resembling hieroglyphs. Researchers have yet to crack the code on this ancient Rapa Nui script. More mysterious items, including an atypical female moai, make it a mind-bending experience.

MANA GALLERY

There are plenty of souvenir craft markets on island, but this striking A-frame gallery is one of the only places where you'll find modern Polynesian art. Collectors stop by for the museum-quality woodcarvings, pearl jewellery, intricate stonework and other artisan goods.

Above: *Discover Polynesian art and artistry at the Mana Gallery;* ***Opposite:*** *Rapa Nui's monolithic moai.*

Above: *Karel Appel's Frog and Cat, Naoshima Island, Japan;*
Opposite: *Ernest Zacharevic street-art piece, George Town, Malaysia.*

ASIA

TOKYO, JAPAN

Contemporary art meets tradition

WHEN TO GO
Tokyo is a year-round destination, with winter seeing fewer crowds. Art exhibitions are often seasonal or tied to the seasons.

GETTING THERE
Haneda (HND) is the more convenient of Tokyo's two international airports. Narita (NRT), in neighbouring Chiba Prefecture, gets most of the budget flights.

Tokyo is the centre of Japan's contemporary art scene, a place to see cutting-edge digital art, pop-culture-inflected installations and street art from Japanese artists, as well as leading international ones. The city's museums are also strong in Japan's traditional arts, from the monochrome ink-wash paintings of the medieval era to the urbane, polychrome prints of the early modern era.

Prominent national museums give a good introduction to the arts and the eras. Smaller, niche museums might focus on just one thing – like kites or the art of the tea ceremony. The museum buildings themselves, often designed by internationally famous architects, are also part of the attraction.

Beyond museums, many of Tokyo's mixed-use complexes and malls – known for their eye-catching architecture – have fantastic public-art installations. There are also plenty of galleries where you can take the pulse of the contemporary art scene, plus regular cultural events like film festivals.

Tokyo doesn't have a singular designated arts district; it's too large and decentralised for that. However, a few places to hone in on include **Ueno** (for traditional art) and **Roppongi** (for contemporary art). But part of the beauty of the Japanese capital is that art is everywhere – if you know where to look.

TOKYO NATIONAL MUSEUM

The nation's oldest museum houses the world's largest collection of Japanese art, spanning from antiquity to the early modern era. Galleries organised by era or craft offer a perfect introduction for visitors with little or no background in the classical arts of Japan, which include scroll paintings, ceramics, lacquerware, calligraphy, Buddhist sculpture and metalwork.

TEAMLAB BORDERLESS

Recently reopened in a new venue, this museum has quickly become one of Tokyo's top attractions. Founded in Tokyo, international art collective teamLab creates immersive, interactive installations that dazzle the senses while pushing the frontiers of art itself. Borderless is just one of teamLab's museums, and it contains over 70 original works.

***Right:** Inside Tokyo's Kite Museum; **Above:** teamLab Borderless' Universe of Water Particles on a Rock Where People Gather; **Opposite:** Gilded Buddha at the Tokyo National Museum.*

Yayoi Kusama Museum

Kusama Yayoi (b 1929) is one of Japan's most internationally famous contemporary artists, particularly known for her obsession with dots and pumpkins. She cut her teeth in New York City's 1950s avant-garde scene and remains prolific today, with tickets to see her work selling out quickly all over the world. Kusama is in possession of many of her works and shows them in rotating gallery exhibitions, and in 2017 she founded the Yayoi Kusama Museum.

Located in the Shinjuku area in Tokyo, the 5-storey building includes a rooftop gallery, and while the levels aren't too spacious, they certainly pack a punch, as one would expect. Fans of the artist's distinctly colourful style can get a glimpse (though limited to a 90-minute visit) of her wildly colourful paintings, polka-dotted pumpkins and mirror-lined infinity rooms. Unlike museums dedicated to a single artist that remain pretty static, the Yayoi Kusama Museum often changes exhibits, which makes the tickets highly coveted, considering even Tokyoites are itching to visit at least twice a year. Also, the museum often exhibits works for the first time ever in Japan – or the world. Tickets must be purchased in advance online and tend to go fast.

TOKYO ART MUSEUMS

Mori Art Museum
Blockbuster contemporary art shows atop a skyscraper

Tokyo Photographic Arts Museum
The place to see photography exhibits in Tokyo

Ōta Memorial Museum of Art
Dedicated to *ukiyo-e*, Japanese woodblock prints

Japan Folk Crafts Museum
Artisan crafts from around Japan in a traditional rural villa

National Museum of Modern Art
MOMAT offers a crash course in Japanese modernism

Nezu Museum
A renowned collection of East Asian antiquities

Hatakeyama Memorial Museum of Fine Art
All about the art of the tea ceremony

Museum of Contemporary Art Tokyo
Japanese artists and movements from the postwar period

Musée Tomo
Among the best collections of contemporary Japanese ceramics

Yamatane Museum of Art
Modern Japanese-style paintings on paper and silk

National Museum of Western Art
Monets and more in a building by Le Corbusier

21_21 DESIGN SIGHT
Cultural institution devoted to design in all forms

Taro Okamoto Memorial Museum
The home-studio of an avant-garde postwar artist

Shunkaen Bonsai Museum
A living garden museum of trees in miniature

Tokyo Metropolitan Teien Art Museum
Decorative arts displayed in an Art Deco imperial villa

National Crafts Museum
Traditional lacquerware, ceramics, bamboo work and more

Asakura Museum of Sculpture
A local favourite, with cat sculptures and traditional architecture

Studio Ghibli Museum
A must for Miyazaki lovers; a theater shows original shorts seen only here

PUBLIC ARTWORKS

Louise Bourgeois, *Maman*
One of the French artist's monumental bronze spider sculptures

Yoshitomo Nara, *Miss Forest*
A garden gnome as envisioned by the pop-punk Japanese artist

Okamoto Taro, *Myth of Tomorrow*
A haunting mural depicting Hiroshima in Shibuya Station

Miyazaki Hayao, *Ni-Tele Really Big Clock*
Working steampunk clock from Japan's master animator

Kohei Nawa, *White Deer*
Majestic example of the Japanese artist's signature deer sculptures

Lee Ufan, *Relatum*
Abstract work in water and stone by the pioneering Korean artist

Roy Lichtenstein, *Tokyo Brushstrokes I & II*
Sinuous sculptures from an icon of modernism on the streets of Shinjuku

Aryz, *The Shamisen*
Multistory mural in vibrant colour by the Spanish street artist

Tokujin Yoshioka, *Star*
Dazzling silver starburst by a Japanese artist captivated by light

Choi Jeong-Hwa, Robo Robo Park
Art meets play at this park designed by the Korean artist

Jaume Plensa, *Roots*
Larger-than-life depiction of the human form in language

Mural City Project Koenji
Street art scattered around a Tokyo counterculture hub

Clockwise from top left: *The sleek abode of 21_21 DESIGN SIGHT; the Tokyo Photographic Arts Museum exterior; Feline the vibes at the Asakura Museum of Sculpture; in the atrium at the Mori Art Museum.*

TOP MUSEUM
東京都写真美術館
TOKYO PHOTOGRAPHIC ART MUSEUM

MORI ART MUSEUM

NAOSHIMA, JAPAN

Art island in the Inland Sea

WHEN TO GO

Combine your trip with cherry blossoms in spring or fall colours in autumn. June–August is hot and humid; November–March is cold.

GETTING THERE

Take a ferry from Uno Port in Okayama Prefecture on Honshū, or from Takamatsu city on Shikoku.

In an unparalleled success story of economic regeneration thanks to investment in arts and culture, Naoshima – described as a 'sad little island' in the 1960s by expat writer Donald Ritchie – has evolved into one of Japan's most popular visitor attractions.

Sitting in Japan's Inland Sea, among some 3000 islands in the calm stretch of waters between Honshū and Shikoku, Naoshima was facing a dim future of depopulation until the Fukutake family and their Benesse Corporation turned things around by transforming the island into an art destination. With support from luminaries such as renowned Japanese architect Tadao Ando and artist Yayoi Kusama, Naoshima has become a landscape of integrated museums and art installations, recognised in art circles worldwide.

This arts-and-culture recipe to revitalise dwindling island communities has been replicated on nearby **Teshima** and **Inujima**. Both islands now also include installations that are part of the wider **Benesse Art Site Naoshima** and are easy to visit on day trips while staying on Naoshima. The island is now a vibrant community; young people from across Japan have relocated to set up businesses and start new lives. Every three years the **Setouchi Trienniale** sees new projects unveiled on Naoshima and surrounding islands.

Right: *Playful spheres by SANAA architects Kazuyo Sejima and Ryue Nishizawa shroud the Naoshima port terminal's cycle pavilion;* ***Opposite:*** *Yayoi Kusama's Yellow Pumpkin, at the Benesse House Museum.*

CHICHŪ ART MUSEUM

This extraordinary building, designed by Tadao Ando, is a series of concrete-walled galleries fitted into a hillside. Natural light filters into the cool caverns to illuminate five of Monet's water lily paintings. Three light installations by James Turrell also feature, along with a monumental set of sculptures by Walter De Maria.

BENESSE HOUSE MUSEUM

This museum and hotel combination, also designed by Ando, features interior and exterior artwork – including art in the hotel rooms. The colourful outdoor pieces are mesmerising, topped off by Yayoi Kusama's famous *Yellow Pumpkin*, which sits at the end of its own pier at the peaceful beach.

Art House Project

Naoshima Island's east-side fishing port of Honmura is filled with narrow lanes of blackened-timber wooden houses, many of which were abandoned over the years as the village suffered depopulation. Benesse stepped in to convert a number of properties – including a Shinto shrine and a Buddhist temple – into art installations, as part of its Art House Project. Visiting them can be an arty treasure hunt as the installations are scattered throughout town, most of them unassuming from the street. Though they may blend into the surrounding traditional neighbourhood, the interiors have been passed over to artists to convert into whatever suits their artistic vision.

The temple **Minamidera** accommodates an ingenious experiment with light by James Turrell. Entering what appears to be a pitch-dark space, visitors sit and wait for their eyes to adjust to the dark to enjoy the artwork. **Go'o Shrine** features a glass staircase leading down to a narrow underground 'stone chamber'. **Haisha**, occupying the former home and office of a local dentist, features playful artwork, including a multistorey, indoor replica of the Statue of Liberty. Lots of cute craft shops and cafes have sprung up along the route to cater to visitors, so take time to explore, whether on foot or by bicycle.

SEOUL, SOUTH KOREA

Contemporary arts hub

WHEN TO GO
April and early May, October and early November offer the best climate. September for the international art fair Frieze Seoul and art fest Kiaf.

GETTING THERE
Incheon International Airport (ICN) is 50km (31 miles) west of Seoul, and an hour away by train.

South Korea is a superstar in the world of contemporary art and culture, with its capital Seoul the epicentre of the nation's creativity. Pulsing with energy and bright ideas, the city's proud history of artistic engagement is evident in everything from the polychromatic decoration of its Joseon-dynasty palaces to the dazzling array of treasures housed in its many museums. A day alone can easily be spent browsing the vast collection at the **National Museum of Korea**. **Seoul Museum of Art (SeMA)** also puts on superb shows at its main gallery and scattered satellite branches, including **Nam June Paik Memorial House**.

However, for most visitors, the most exciting draws of Seoul's artistic scene are to be found in its abundance of modern and contemporary works. Thanks to city ordinances and planning policies, there's a wealth of **public art** – check out giant sculptures such as Jonathan Borofsky's 22m-tall (72ft) *Hammering Man* and Claes Oldenburg's *Spring*, striking against the backdrop of the Cheong-gye-cheon stream. A defunct car-park ramp behind Seoul Station houses the site-specific artworks of **Docking Seoul**. And in neighbourhoods such as **Ihwa Maeul** and **Mullae-dong**, wander through alleys daubed with extraordinary murals.

***Below:** Goryeo Dynasty stone pagoda from Gyeongcheonsa temple site, in the National Museum of Korea; **Left:** Central Seoul's Cheonggyecheon Stream, illuminated for the city's Lantern Festival.*

LEEUM MUSEUM OF ART

Elegantly designed and arranged, this Samsung Foundation of Culture–run institution balances traditional Korean art with modern and contemporary works. A trio of celebrated architects (Mario Botta, Jean Nouvel and Rem Koolhaas) participated in the construction. The exhibitions journey from Goryeo- and Joseon-dynasty works – including painting, calligraphy and ceramics – to the 20th-century creations of Korean standout creatives such as Nam June Paik and Kim Whan-ki.

SEOUL MUSEUM OF CRAFT ART

Housed in a former high school and adjoining new buildings, this splendid museum showcases gorgeous crafts, ranging from Joseon-dynasty ceramics, metalwork and mother-of-pearl lacquerware to folding screens of embroidered birds and flowers.

Nam June Paik & MMCA

Seoul was the birthplace of Nam June Paik (1932–2006), a pioneer of video art. A visionary who embraced mass media and new technology, Paik coined the phrase 'electronic superhighway' in 1974. **Nam June Paik Memorial House** is a small gallery devoted to his works and based in a converted *hanok*, a traditional Korean home similar to the one that the artist grew up in. Among his most impressive pieces is *The More, The Better,* a tower of cathode-ray TVs screening different videos, that dominates the atrium of the **National Museum of Modern and Contemporary Art** (MMCA) in Gwacheon, a short subway ride south of the city.

For more contemporary creativity head to the MMCA's main Seoul branch in the artsy neighbourhood of **Bukcheon**. This large complex combines spacious modern galleries with the repurposed red-brick buildings of the former Defense Security Command. Past exhibitions at the venue have focused on the impact of gaming and virtual-reality technologies on Korean art. MMCA Seoul also hosts the annual Korea Artist Prize, which provides an illuminating overview of the local contemporary art scene. Near to the MMCA, also dip into some of Seoul's top commercial galleries, including **Gallery Hyundai**, **Hakgojae** and **Kukje**.

BEIJING, CHINA

Art reinvented in an ancient capital

WHEN TO GO
April–May and September–October, escaping winter cold and summer crowds.

GETTING THERE
Beijing's twin airports – Capital (PEK) and Daxing (PKX) – bring in flights from across the globe; explore the city by taxi or on the Beijing Subway.

Newcomers to China might expect to find artistic expression stifled by the state, but creativity abounds inside the People's Republic. There's censorship, certainly, and social codes that can be just as tricky for artists to navigate, but also a lavish history of painting, sculpture, music, poetry, song and dance spanning four millennia, alongside dynamic modern movements in art and design.

The capital of China since 1279, Beijing is the pulsing heart of the Chinese art scene, and commercial galleries are opening at breakneck speed as the middle classes flex their art-buying muscles. It's fascinating to contrast the state-approved view of art at the **National Art Museum of China** with the effusive creativity on show in spaces such as the postindustrial **UCCA Center for Contemporary Art**.

Exhibitions were once concentrated in artists' quarters, such as the legendary **798 Art District** and the now-demolished Caochangdi Art District – former home of Ai Weiwei's studio – but today galleries are diffusing through the city. Swing by central spots such as **Today Art Museum** or surprising exhibition spaces in the burbs like the garden-ringed **Red Brick Art Museum** – you'll find work that transcends expectations, making challenging statements about China's changing identity.

NATIONAL ART MUSEUM OF CHINA

Slip into a world of ethereal hand-scroll paintings, intricate calligraphy, Communist iconography and ambitious modern expression at the largest art museum in China. While controversial topics are rarely tackled, you'll find everything from art photography to 1000-year-old Buddhas, in a landmark campus close to the Forbidden City.

UCCA CENTER FOR CONTEMPORARY ART

Part of the hip and happening 798 Art District, this boundary-pushing art museum was founded in 2007 and is still one of the best places to take the pulse of the Beijing art scene. Exhibitions and public events always lead somewhere interesting.

Left: *The Ming Dynasty Beijing Qingming Scroll, displayed at the National Art Museum of China;*
Above: *Cao Fei's Staging the Era show at UCCA;*
Opposite: *The National Art Museum facade;*
Next spread: *UCCA's 15th anniversary exhibition.*

Stray
Alchemists

王拓
空手走入历史
WANG TUO
EMPTY-HANDED
INTO HISTORY

ELIZABETH PEYTON:
PRACTICE

RAUSCHENBERG IN CHINA

喻红
金色天景
YU HONG
GOLDEN
SKY

Huang Rui

张元：有种

刘小东：
金城小子
LIU
XIAODONG:
HOMETOWN
BOY

刘小东
Liu
Xiaodong
你的朋友
Your Friends
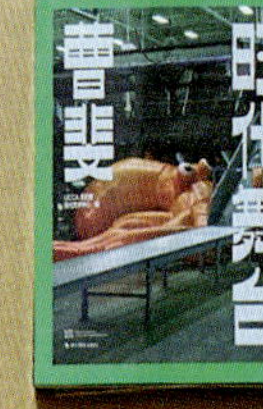

'85
NEW WAVE
新潮
UCCA
THE BIRTH OF CHINESE CONTEMPORARY ART

'85
NEW WAVE
新潮
UCCA

NASA Says It Has Found
The Most 'Earth-Like'
Planet Yet

YELLOW
SIGNAL
WANG
JIAN
WEI

QIU ZHIJIE

VOICE
FOR
MY
FATHER
Yan Pei-Ming
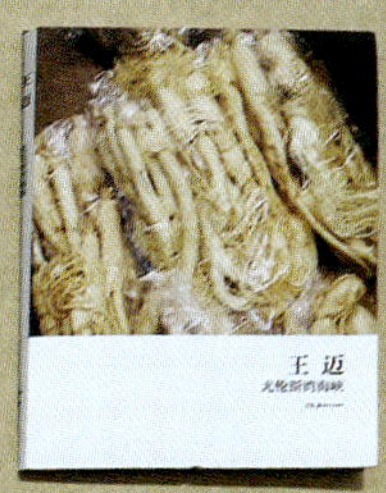
王迈
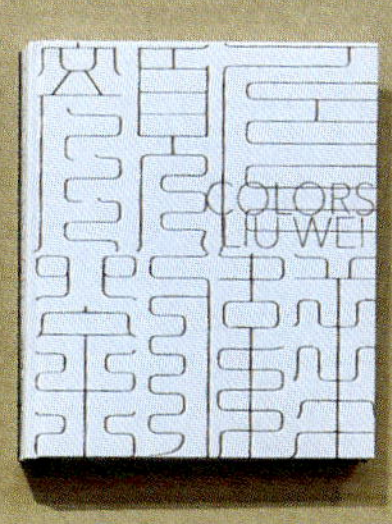
COLORS
LIU WEI

郝量
潇湘八景

沈远：
急促的话语
SHEN YUAN:
HURRIED
WORDS

沃霍尔
ANDY
WARHOL

he stones
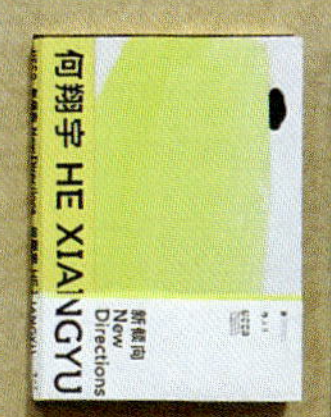
何翔宇 HE XIANGYU
New Directions

陶辉 TAO HUI
New Directions

郝敬班 HAO JINGBAN
New Directions

DAVID DIAO

占卜者之屋
黄永砯回顾展

文明
CIVILIZATION

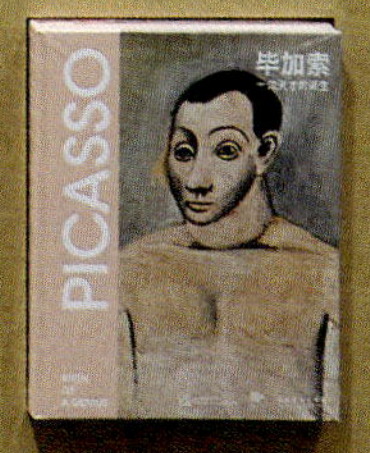
PICASSO
毕加索
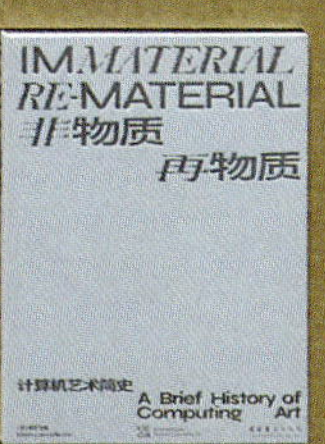
IMMATERIAL
RE-MATERIAL
非物质
再物质
计算机艺术简史
A Brief History of Computing Art

GANG

BENTU
本土

A18

A factory for creativity

There's no better metaphor for the journey of Beijing's art scene than the **798 Art District** in Dashanzi. Founded in 1951 as part of the Socialist Unification partnership between China and the Soviet Union, this once-gloomy factory complex was originally part of China's military-industrial facility, but has blossomed into a hub for contemporary art.

Conceived by Russian, Chinese and East German engineers, these functional blocks were adorned with Communist slogans in red Chinese characters, reminding the thousands who worked here (producing electronics) of their grand social mission. The slogans remain today, fading slowly on the ceiling arches above eclectic works of modern art.

Having fallen into a slow decline in the late 1980s, the complex began its phoenixlike renaissance in 1995, when the **Central Academy of Fine Arts** set up a workshop in Factory 706. More creatives followed – first sculptor Sui Jianguo, then a flood of artists and designers – including Huang Rui of the avant-garde **Stars Art Group** – who put the 798 Art District on the map.

Today, the complex has become Beijing's most dynamic art address, alive with workshops, studios, exhibition spaces, shops, bars and cafes, alongside prestigious art institutions like the UCCA Center for Contemporary Art. Make a day of it and see what you discover...

KATHMANDU, NEPAL

Art meets artistry in the shadow of the Himalayas

WHEN TO GO
October to November and March to May, avoiding winter chills and summer rains.

GETTING THERE
Tribhuvan International Airport (KTM) is less than an hour from Kathmandu's historic heart; explore on foot or by taxi.

In Nepal's atmospheric capital, creativity is intertwined with spirituality and religious devotion. Kathmandu is a city that is constantly creating – you'll see artisans hammering out intricate repousse metalwork at the roadsides, carpenters chiselling deities into the timbers of Hindu temples, and novice monks painting intricate mandalas in the courtyards of Buddhist monasteries.

But don't be fooled into thinking that Kathmandu's art scene only looks to the past. Thanks to patronage from local philanthropists and international organisations, contemporary art is flourishing, with many of the city's most talented creatives taking up residency at the **Kathmandu Art House** – founded by the owners of one of Kathmandu's first backpacker hotels.

Talents such as Asha Dangol are fusing themes from Hindu and Buddhist religious art with powerful modern messages about politics, development, inequality and the environment. Shows pop up everywhere, from backpacker cafes to high-end art spaces, such as the **Museum of Nepali Art (MoNA)** and **Siddhartha Art Gallery**.

Discover traditional art forms in the Kathmandu Valley's artisan districts. The lanes around **Bodhnath** are dotted with monastery schools producing *thangkas* (Buddhist cloth paintings) and hammered-metalwork workshops, while **Thimi** and **Bhaktapur** are famed for ceramics. **Patan** is a major centre for lost-wax bronze casting.

SIDDHARTHA ART GALLERY

One of Kathmandu's most respected art spaces, the Siddhartha Art Gallery is the pride of Baber Mahal Revisited – a chic gathering of shops, cafes and cultural spaces in a former royal palace. The gallery has been hosting works in all styles and media since 1987, and gala openings attract Nepal's movers and shakers.

MUSEUM OF NEPALI ART (MoNA)

The first permanent gallery for Nepali contemporary art, MoNA was founded by Rajan Sakya, CEO of the Kathmandu Guest House hotel. Inside, you can view a constantly evolving collection spanning the spectrum of Nepali creativity, from modernist paintings and pop art to traditional art forms created by master artisans.

Above: *Ceramic artists at work in Kathmandu's Bhaktapur district;* ***Opposite:*** *Take in a changing collection of Nepalese art at the city's Museum of Nepali Art (MoNA).*

The house that art built

Tucked into a Thamel backstreet, the **Kathmandu Art House** tied a firework to the tail of the Kathmandu art scene and set it loose. The brainchild of hotelier and art museum director Rajan Sakya, this innovative space behind the Kathmandu Guest House aims to showcase not only the results of Nepali creativity, but also the process.

From humble beginnings in 2021, the Art House has grown into one of Kathmandu's most inspiring creative hubs, providing studio spaces occupied by everyone from hyperrealistic painters to sculptors, tattooists and master craftspeople producing exquisite *paubhas* (Nepali cloth paintings).

Visitors are welcome to wander from studio to studio, discovering what local artists are working on and chatting about the creative process. You may spot visiting dignitaries too – ambassadors and mountaineers often swing by to commission work from artists linked to the Art House and the affiliated Museum of Nepali Art.

If painters Asha Dangol, Erina Tamrakar or Kiran Manandhar are in attendance, drop by to discuss their sources of inspiration, or investigate the almost photographic black-and-white portraits of Manish Dhoju or the Basquiat-like canvases of millennial painter Arnav Man Singh. Check the schedule for special workshops, covering everything from lost-wax casting to Nepali painting styles.

MUMBAI, INDIA

Maximum art in the Maximum City

WHEN TO GO

October to February, avoiding the summer monsoon and spring heat.

GETTING THERE

Mumbai's busy Chhatrapati Shivaji Maharaj International Airport (BOM) has excellent connections worldwide; get around by taxi, suburban train or the Metro.

India's capital of film, fashion and finance is also a vibrant and eclectic centre for the arts, and it's easy to plug into the Mumbai art scene thanks to **Kala Ghoda**, setting for India's largest festival of the arts. Visit this small, central district at festival time and you can tune into everything from poetry readings to painting workshops and movie screenings.

Mumbai is also the city that birthed the influential **Bombay School**, spearheaded by students from the **Sir JJ School of Art**, where Rudyard Kipling's father was a professor. Painters such as Pestonji Bomanji injected Indian soul into European-influenced observational art, while FN Souza and other members of the post-Independence **Bombay Progressive Artists' Group** strived for a distinctively Indian form of modern expression.

Shows linked to graduates of the 'JJ School' still draw appreciative crowds, and standout works from the Bombay School are displayed in big-name venues such as the **Jehangir Art Gallery** and **Jehangir Nicholson Art Foundation**. But increasingly, the focus is on smaller, more intimate spaces. The popular traveller hub of Colaba fizzes with boundary-pushing galleries such as **Chatterjee & Lal**, **Akara Art** and **Experimenter Colaba**, while nearby Fort hosts the prestigious **Chemould Prescott Road** gallery.

KALA GHODA

While new art events, such as the Art Mumbai fair in November, are drawing fanfare, the red-letter date on the creative calendar is the long-established Kala Ghoda Arts Festival. Paintings, sculpture, music, film and the spoken word have filled the lanes of the Khala Ghoda district between Fort and Colaba every February since 1999.

DAG MUMBAI

The Mumbai branch of Delhi Art Gallery (DAG) is the place to gaze on 18th-, 19th- and 20th-century Indian artworks, with regular exhibitions spread over an elegant space inside the iconic Taj Mahal Palace hotel. Look out for shows featuring the work of national luminaries such as Jamini Roy and FN Souza.

***Above:** The Taj Mahal Palace in Colaba, home to the galleries of DAG Mumbai;* ***Opposite:** Interactive art on show during the Kala Ghoda Festival.*

The art of film

Mumbai's famous film industry is not just one art form, but many, and day trips to **Mumbai Filmcity** (Dadasaheb Phalke Chitranagari), **SJ Studios** and other cogs in the Bollywood machine offer a chance to go behind the scenes of India's all-singing, all-dancing movie extravaganzas.

Worth a staggering US$2.28 billion per year, Bollywood supports an entire ecosystem of filmmakers, actors, designers, costume-makers, stylists, dancers, choreographers and more. Soundtrack composers such as Sameer Anjaan and AR Rahman are some of the most prolific music artists on the planet, and sitting in on a song-and-dance number is a key part of a studio tour.

Even the theatre end of the movie business supports a legion of poster artists, though the old-timers who once hand-painted billboards in front of iconic Art Deco cinemas (such as the Eros, Regal and Liberty) are being eased out by hip young graphic designers with laptops and cutting-edge software.

Then there's the fashion industry that dresses the stars in glittering bridal *lehanga* gowns and *sherwani* jackets. Visit Mumbai during **Fashion Week** in March and you'll see the work of India's top designers being sported on and off the catwalk, and maybe get within selfie-snapping distance of some Bollywood A-listers.

BANGKOK, THAILAND

An expressive legacy

WHEN TO GO
November to February promises peak comfortable weather – also, peak travellers, but Bangkok's crowded, anyway.

GETTING THERE
Bangkok's Suvarnabhumi (BKK) is Southeast Asia's busiest airport, with plenty of direct US and Europe connections.

In Thailand's capital, art is everywhere you turn. The local culture's deep respect for artistic expression stems from collective values that place beauty and worldliness as inherently sacred. As such, royal and religious architecture are multifaceted masterworks – Bangkok's famous **Grand Palace** blends vibrant Khmer- and Chinese-style cultural and artistic influences in its shrines and statues with European- and Renaissance-revival building majesty.

On a modern note, Thailand's artistry of today extends far beyond its origins of fine handicraft and artisanship. Bangkok is truly one of the world's most exciting cities for contemporary art. There are fantastic public urban installations and private galleries galore (these are also often free to visit). Meanwhile, a cool underground scene emerging in disused shophouses provides a space for young Thai to create, in spite of government censorship.

Get up close and personal with artists and also their works at the **Bangkok Art and Culture Center (BACC)**, a 3000-sq-metre (32, 292-sq-ft) powerhouse of commercial galleries and ateliers, as well as **Chatuchak Weekend Market**'s hangar art section. Also not to miss: graffiti-covered lanes in Chinatown's **Talat Noi** neighbourhood, as well as the edgy 'creative park' **Chang Chui**, featuring gigantic installations and artist studios.

BANGKOK ART & CULTURE CENTRE (BACC)

The Bangkok Art and Culture Centre sprawls across three levels, encompassing commercial galleries and an art library, as well as imaginative cafes and boutiques (head to the Ice-DEA shop for so-called designer ice cream). Check the BACC website for a busy programme of free cultural performances and events.

NATIONAL MUSEUM

Thailand's National Museum is mostly focused on history, but also provides a perfect walk through the country's rich artistic legacy. Here, in one of Southeast Asia's largest museums, discover a vast collection of cultural and religious artefacts, across ancient times and Bangkok's 18th century – for example, beautiful textile and ceramic works, Buddhist iconography and more.

Right: *The Bhuddhaisawan Chapel at the National Museum;* ***Above:*** *Street art in the Talat Noi district of Bangkok's Chinatown;* ***Opposite:*** *A snapshot of the BACC's recurring White Elephant exhibition.*

Thailand Creative & Design Center (TCDC)

In recent years, Bangkok's contemporary arts scene has enjoyed a real renaissance, spearheaded by ambitious young Thai creators with a passion for art, fashion and design. In ageing commercial pockets around Old Bangkok, especially Chinatown, disused shophouses and warehouses are being renovated into spiffy new spaces showcasing their unique styles and passion.

The Thailand Creative & Design Centre (TCDC) is the home turf where these young creatives come together to network, be inspired and share ideas. The gorgeous Art Deco building, in the historic Silom neighbourhood, is partially occupied by Bangkok's main post office. But in 2005, a hefty, 9000-sq-metre (96,875-sq-ft) chunk of the building was renovated into a public resource centre for Bangkok's design and creative industry.

The 'creative incubator' is a slick, modern space of five storeys, with much to lay eyes on. Books and magazines are laid out in an art- and design-heavy research library, and structurally stunning collaborative workspaces. Come by and snap a few social-media pics of the archival area and on-site gallery, and take in the view from the top-floor cafe and rooftop terrace. TCDC is free to visit and makes for a lovely (and air conditioned!) pit stop when exploring Bangkok's historic riverside area.

PENANG, MALAYSIA

Malaysian street-art hotspot

WHEN TO GO

It's hot and humid year-round. The George Town Literary Festival is held at the end of November.

GETTING THERE

Fly into Penang International Airport (PEN). Penang's train station is in Butterworth, on the mainland of peninsula Malaysia.

George Town, the capital of the Malaysian state of Penang, is a city of arty good looks. Its UNESCO World Heritage–listed central core is like an architectural jewel box of ornate, multihued heritage shophouses, temples and Chinese clan houses. Overlaying this is an abundance of **street art**, adding a vibrant and contemporary edge.

Penang's love of street art goes back to 2010 when the state government commissioned a series of three-dimensional steel-art cartoon caricatures detailing aspects of the island's rich history and culture. But it was the appearance on a wall of *Two Kids on a Bicycle*, a mixed-media piece by Lithuanian artist Ernest Zacharevic for the 2012 George Town Festival, that was the flame that set alight the scene. That mural – and others by Zacharevic – number among Penang's most iconic images.

Other under-the-radar art gems around Penang including the **Witness Collection**, an appointment-only gallery of contemporary works mainly from Vietnam and Cambodia; and **Art and Garden by Fuan Wong**, a local glass-artist's open-air studio where sculptures and installations are mixed with an amazing collection of tropical plants.

Right: *Striking a balletic pose at the Hin Bus Depot contemporary arts centre;* ***Opposite:*** *Ernest Zacharevic's Two Kids on a Bicycle, which kickstarted George Town's street-art explosion.*

HIN BUS DEPOT

Built in 1947, the Hin Bus Depot began to morph into its current guise as George Town's contemporary arts hub in 2014. The ruined shell of this handsome Art Deco building provided the perfect backdrop for street art and, following a successful exhibition by Ernest Zacharevic, it became a permanent base for local creatives.

BATIK PAINTING MUSEUM PENANG

In the 1940s, the Penang-based artist Chuah Thean Teng (1914–2008) began experimenting with batik. Several of his distinctive canvases can be viewed at this small museum in the heart of George Town's heritage zone, along with those of around 25 other batik-painting artists.

SINGAPORE, SINGAPORE

Creative city-state

Since it began to develop as a major international port in the early 19th century, Singapore has been a place where art and ideas from widely different cultures have mixed and mingled. Look to the hybrid culture of Peranakans (descendants of immigrants and local Malay people) to see how this has creatively played out in everything from architecture and interior design to fashion.

The island state may be nicknamed the 'Little Red Dot', but its promotion of the arts gains it a big red checkmark on any list of art-focused destinations. Alongside the splendid **National Gallery**, **Asian Civilisations Museum (ACM)** and **Singapore Art Museum (SAM)** there are scores of smaller galleries and cultural spaces, such as the contemporary art galleries of **Gillman Barracks**, a former British military encampment transformed into an arts hub.

There's also plentiful public art. Marc Quinn's *Planet*, a 10m-long (33ft) sculpture of a baby, hovers over a field in the space-age **Gardens by the Bay**, while the nearby **ArtScience Museum** blooms like a giant concrete flower. Street art brightens the walls of the **Kampong Glam**, **Katong** and **Chinatown** neighbourhoods – in the latter search out Yip Yew Chong's heritage-inspired murals, including his 44m-long (144ft) piece at the Thian Hock Keng Temple.

WHEN TO GO

In mid-January for Singapore Art Week (nac.gov.sg/artweek) and early November for the Affordable Art Fair.

GETTING THERE

Changi Airport (SIN) is a regional air hub. There are also buses and trains to neighbouring Malaysia and ferries to nearby Indonesian islands.

Below: Inside one of the biodomes at the fantastical Gardens by the Bay; **Left:** Marc Quinn's Planet; **Next spread:** Natural planting surrounds the biodomes, skywalks and 'supertrees' at the Gardens by the Bay.

NATIONAL GALLERY SINGAPORE

Home to the world's largest public collection of Singaporean and Southeast Asian modern art, this splendid gallery occupies a building that once housed the City Hall and Supreme Court. The permanent collection ranges from historical works – 19th-century botanical watercolours and paintings by seminal local artists such as Liu Kang (1911–2004) – to more contemporary pieces like Lee Wen's art photograph *Journey of a Yellow Man No. 11: Multi-Culturalism*.

ASIAN CIVILISATIONS MUSEUM (ACM)

Occupying the neoclassical Empress Place Building, completed in 1897, this fine ethnographic and decorative arts museum presents the region's most comprehensive collection of Pan-Asian treasures. There are three thematic floors – Maritime Trade, Faith and Belief, and Materials and Design.

MANILA, PHILIPPINES

Art with a metropolitan edge

WHEN TO GO
January to April, for dry skies.

GETTING THERE
Flights drop into Ninoy Aquino International Airport (MNL) in the southern suburbs; reach the galleries by commuter train, bus, taxi or jeepney.

At one time, the Filipino capital was better known for papermaking than artwork creating, but that's a view from another century. Young, expressive Filipino artists have transformed Metro Manila into one of Asia's most dynamic centres for contemporary art, aided by strong cultural links to the art scene in the US.

Some of the best-loved Manila artworks are city-commissioned murals and sculptures celebrating the Philippines' struggle for independence. Public pieces such as Eduardo Castrillo's *Katipunan Revolution Monument* and Botong Francisco's *Filipino Struggles Through History* murals are cultural landmarks, fusing revolutionary themes with Asian and international art sensibilities.

But increasingly, the public art baton has passed to avant-garde street artists, helped by initiatives such as the **Filipino Street Art Project** and the growing profile of mural artists, such as Kris Abrigo, Brayan Barrios and the politically charged Ang Gerilya collective.

The gallery scene is thriving too, fuelled by an explosion of art spaces in Manila's ultramodern metros – exemplified by **Silverlens**, **Ateneo Art Gallery**, **ArtInformal** and **Modeka Art**. For an overview of Manila's art evolution, take in revered national artists at the **National Museum** and **Metropolitan Museum**, then discover contemporary talent at the **Pintô Art Museum** on the city fringes.

NATIONAL MUSEUM

The National Museum campus at Rizal Park covers everything from anthropology to natural history, but it's the fine arts department that catches attention. Here, you'll see panels from Botong Francisco's *Filipino Struggles Through History* murals as well as the work of national icons such as painters Félix Resurrección Hidalgo and Juan Luna and sculptor Guillermo Tolentino.

PINTÔ ART MUSEUM

Set in an eye-catching, Spanish-inspired building in the satellite city of Antipolo, the Pintô was the brainchild of Manila doctor and art patron Joven Cuanang. Built to showcase the work of the Salingpusa art collective, it's a great spot to discover contemporary artists and the sense of community underpinning the Filipino art scene.

Above: *The Pintô Art Museum in Antipolo, just outside of Manila;* ***Opposite:*** *Eduardo Castrillo's Katipunan Revolution Monument, one of many public artworks dotted around the city.*

Above: *Atelier Cézanne, Aix-en-Provence, France;*
Opposite: *Antoni Gaudí's Casa Vicens, Barcelona, Spain.*

EUROPE

REYKJAVÍK & BEYOND, ICELAND

Edgy art and creatively crafty wares

WHEN TO GO

Reykjavík is fabulous year-round. For midnight sun, travel June–July; for the northern lights, visit September–April.

GETTING THERE

Fly into Keflavík International Airport (KEF), 49km (30 miles) southwest of Reykjavík. Buses to Reykjavík coordinate with flight schedules.

Captivating sculptures enrich Reykjavík's streets. Jón Gunnar Árnason's ship-like *Sun Voyager* (*Sólfar*) arcs alongside the bay. Near Lake Tjörnin, bump into Magnús Tómasson's *The Unknown Bureaucrat*, a sculpture of a man being crushed by a rock; and *The Black Cone*, an ode to peaceful civil disobedience by Santiego Sierra. The work of female Icelandic sculptors is highlighted in **Hljómskálagarður Park**.

Galleries such as **i8** exhibit some of the country's top working artists. They share their Grandi location in the Marshall House with gallery **Kling og Bang** and artist-run exhibition space **Nýló** (Living Art Museum).

The **Reykjavík Museum of Photography** vies for attention with sculpture specialists **Sigurjón Ólafsson Museum** and **Einar Jónsson Museum**, the latter with a free sculpture garden in the shadow of famed Hallgrimskirkja. Head to **Viðey Island** for giant installations by Richard Serra and Yoko Ono.

There's more to see if you journey into the rest of Iceland. In thenorth, Akureyri's museum, **Listasafnið á Akureyri**, features avant-garde Icelandic art, past and present, while the **Icelandic Folk and Outsider Art Museum** is lined with quirky art. In the northeast, discover the enthralling massive stone gates of **Arctic Henge**.

In the Westfjords, don't miss **Samúel Jónsson's Art Museum**, enchanting cartoonlike sculptures and buildings at the farthest end of magnificent Arnarfjörður.

REYKJAVÍK ART MUSEUM

The country's largest art institution fills three locations. The central Hafnarhús is in a warehouse converted into a soaring steel-and-concrete exhibition space near the waterfront in Old Reykjavík. Cutting-edge contemporary Icelandic art changes frequently – expect installations, videos, paintings and sculpture, plus the comic-book-style work of political artist Erró (Guðmundur Guðmundsson). Create an art walk using the Reykjavík Art Walk mobile app.

THE FACTORY, DJÚPAVÍK

Navigate mountain roads with fjord views to the enchanting derelict factory at Djúpavík – all crumbling plaster, towering chimneys and vast water tanks. Summer exhibitions can include photos, paintings, fabrics, found art, sculpture or installations, blending with the sounds of the waterfall and waves outside.

Above: *Alexander Stirling Calder's statue of Viking explorer Leifur Eiríksson presides over Reykjavík's Hallgrimskirkja;* ***Opposite:*** *The summer art exhibition within the derelict factory at Djúpavík.*

National

Craftwork

Throughout Reykjavík and Iceland you'll find the fruit of Icelandic creativity and craftwork.

In the capital, for example, **Kron** creates handmade shoes, while **Stígur** and **Aurum** make delicate jewellery. Design shops **Kirsuberjatréð** and **Skúmaskot** serve as art cooperatives, grouping talented Icelandic makers of leatherware (some working with fishskin), porcelain, fashion and more. **Fischersund**, in the former recording studio of Icelandic musician Jónsi, is a collective making perfumes, soaps and visual art.

The **Handknitting Association of Iceland** in central Reykjavík has traditional sweaters (called *lopapeysa*), hats, socks and scarves. **Steinunn**, in the Grandi neighbourhood, features a knitted couture collection. The casual-craft spectrum fills the weekend flea market **Kolaportið**.

Knitters can buy yarn, needles and knitting patterns at the Handknitting Association or at **Álafoss**, in a traditional wool mill in Mosfellsbær, just north of Reykjavík. And you'll often find a knitting section at supermarkets, even if just a shelf of local wools in a back corner.

To get a little guidance, book a multiday knitting tour with designer **Hélène Magnússon** (icelandicknitter.com), where you can learn about Icelandic spinning, wool dyeing and garment design, then go hiking and even hear a little folklore. Or plan an experience with **Creative Iceland** – perhaps a workshop in knitting, wool-working, ceramics or knifemaking.

OSLO, NORWAY

Munch magic among the fjords

WHEN TO GO
Oslo is rarely crowded, but avoid peak summer for better deals and fewer crowds. Spring and early autumn are ideal.

GETTING THERE
Oslo Airport (OSL) operates direct flights to European cities, plus several destinations in the US, Asia and Middle East.

Nature works on an epic scale in Oslo, which sits astride the dark, moody Oslofjord, where Vikings once set sail. Here forests ripple away to hills and mountains. Whether seen in winter snow under a rave of northern lights or in the never-dying midsummer sun, this city is intimately in tune with the outdoors. And just as nature ramps up the drama, so too do artists hailing from these Nordic parts, most notably expressionist Edvard Munch (1863–1944), whose trippy *The Scream* sent shockwaves through the art world at a time when most folk were still absorbed with Art Nouveau.

However, Oslo isn't a one-artist wonder. Once you've romped through a lifetime of Munch at the **National Museum** and at **MUNCH** in the revamped Bjørvika port district, as well as visiting **Ekeley**, his beloved former home and studios, it's time for a brush with the Norwegian capital's more progressive cultural side. From the Damien Hirst and Jeff Koons originals at fjord-embracing, Renzo Piano–designed **Astrup Fearnley Museet** to open-air **Vigelandsparken**, showing off more than 200 granite and bronze sculptures by homegrown legend Gustav Vigeland (1869–1943), art and nature here are as one.

MUNCH

In the strikingly revitalised Bjørvika docks, this 13-floor, modern-day 'leaning tower' – designed by Spanish starchitects estudio Herreros – wows with the world's biggest Munch collection: a staggering 1100 paintings and 4500 watercolours. Dive deep into the life of an experimental, ever-innovative artist.

NASJONALMUSEET (NATIONAL MUSEUM)

This vast, showstopping museum delivers an overwhelming collection of art, decorative arts and design under one ecofriendly Kleihues + Schuwerk–designed roof. Inspired by ancient Greek architecture, the luminous Light Hall at the top is a magnificent space for rotating exhibitions of contemporary art, but make a beeline for Room 060 and Munch's *The Scream* (1893), the most impressive of four versions on display in Oslo.

Left: *The waterfront Munch museum, dedicated to Oslo's most famous artist;* ***Above:*** *A bird's-eye view of the city's Nasjonalmuseet (National Museum);* ***Opposite:*** *Inside the Nasjonalmuseet.*

The nature of Munch

It is no secret that Edvard Munch battled the demons of mental illness, suffering from anxiety and hallucinations – and these struggles surface in his one-of-a-kind paintings, with their psychedelic colours, their rapid, swirling brushstrokes, and their ghoulish, madly-staring gaunt figures. But nature provided a refuge for the artist's restless and troubled soul, and is reflected in all its changing moods and lights in his work.

Ekebergparken is where Munch found inspiration for *Skrik* (*The Scream*) while out walking with two friends. Today, you can walk to the hill that inspired this seminal work (now the Munch Spot), as well as hunt for sculptures by Rodin, Renoir, Botero, Bourgeois and Dalí among the woods.

For a deeper exploration, visit Munch's former home and studios at **Ekeley** on the fringes of Oslo, where the artist lived a hermitic existence for the last 28 years of his life, from 1916 to 1944, and where you can stroll the grounds and outdoor areas. Here he sought solace in nature and painted prolifically. His surroundings profoundly informed his art in vibrant colour and motif, from horses ploughing the fields at harvest time to spring in the elm woods. Sit in the fruit orchards to imagine the artist at his easel.

HELSINKI, FINLAND

Fresh art and design on the Baltic coast

WHEN TO GO
Summer brings a raft of art festivals and exhibitions, but less-crowded spring and autumn can be pleasant.

GETTING THERE
Helsinki-Vantaa Airport (HEL) operates flights to numerous European cities and some destinations in America, Asia and the Middle East.

There is Nordic magic in the air in Helsinki. Sitting on a peninsula that projects into the Gulf of Finland and the piercing blue Baltic, swinging between extremes of long, dark winters and eternally light midsummer sun, and defined by its east-meets-west geography – the Finnish capital moves from urban culture to great outdoors without missing a beat.

With forests and lakes right on the doorstep, Helsinki's natural backdrop provides not only plenty of fresh air but also inspiration. Culturally progressive, green-minded and refreshingly quirky, Helsinki entices with an art scene as hot as its saunas. You can spend days roaming museums and galleries that wing you from European Old Masters to 1950s Finnish 'golden age' architecture, contemporary design, punchy Marimekko fashion and transformative, experience-focused art. And when you tire of exhibition halls, heading outdoors for an invigorating walk unravels some sensational public art, with 500 outdoor sculptures and environmental artworks to discover.

More, you say? An hour's drive west reveals treasures: from emotive Ekenäs' **Chappe Art House by the Sea**, to **Fiskars**, an entire village of artists, designers and makers crackling with on-the-pulse creativity.

AMOS REX

Propelling you from the 1930s functionalist Lasipalatsi building to the space age, Amos Rex opened in Helsinki in 2018. At ground level, giant white-tiled, skylight portholes bubble up from undulating concrete and kids skateboard. Subterranean galleries present experimental exhibitions that consider art through emotions – from ecstasy to nostalgia.

CHAPPE, EKENÄS

An hour's drive west of Helsinki, the town of Ekenäs is home to Chappe, Art House by the Sea. The black-timber gallery is the brainchild of late cancer-research scientists and art lovers Albert de la Chapelle and Clara Bloomfield. The exhibitions aim to push boundaries and 'touch the soul'.

Above: *Amos Rex, a splash of the contemporary in central Helsinki;* ***Opposite:*** *Head east of the city to Ekenäs for boundary-pushing exhibitions at Chappe.*

FISKARS
VALIO SIEMEN
UTSÄDE

Fiskars: forging art from iron

Bounded by a gentle river and framed by forests and lakes, Fiskars is a handsome vision of brick-built industrial houses and workers' cottages. An hour's drive west of Helsinki, the nature-immersed village grew up around its ironworks, which opened its doors in 1649. Fast forward a few centuries to 1967 and it was at the cutting edge of design when it launched the world's first orange-plastic-handled scissors. But when sales boomed and the factories moved out of town to bigger premises in the 1980s, Fiskars temporarily lost its spark. Cue Ingmar Lindberg, development director of the Fiskars Corporation, who turned it into an artists' colony, inviting some of Helsinki's finest artists, designers and makers to live and work here.

Today, the community of Fiskars is home to dozens of galleries and studios, many affiliated with the artists' cooperative Onoma, whose 143 active members range from goldsmiths to glassblowers.

The village's summer **biennale** (from mid-June to early September) is when exhibitions of local art enliven the atmospheric warehouses and workrooms of the old ironworks. Year-round **Kupru Galleria** showcases exhibitions by Onoma members, and the **Onoma Shop** is stocked with one-of-a-kind gifts and crafts that bring a dash of art to the everyday.

MUSEUMS

Arkkitehtuurimuseo
This outstanding museum illuminates Finnish architecture from 1900 to 1970, winging you from classicism to functionalism and modernism

Ateneum Art Museum
In a neo-Renaissance building, this gallery shines a light on 'golden age' Finnish paintings and sculptures, from the late 19th century to the 1950s

Helsinki Art Museum (HAM)
Presents an astounding romp through 20th- and 21st-century Finnish art in the 1930s Tennispalatsi (Tennis Palace)

Kansallismuseo
In a Romantic/Art Nouveau building, the National Museum forces you to look up in wonder at ceiling frescoes of the Finnish epic *Kalevala,* painted by Akseli Gallen-Kallela

Kiasma
Designed by American architect Steven Holl, this eye-catching metallic curve of a gallery unveils an exciting collection of Finnish and international contemporary art

Kunsthalle Helsinki
Here the spotlight is on contemporary art, with rotating exhibitions galloping from graffiti art to Hockney's iPad works

Sinebrychoffin Taidemuseo
The lavish, chandelier-lit offices of a wealthy brewing family have been reborn as Helsinki's foremost collection of classic European paintings, with an emphasis on Old Masters and portrait miniatures

PUBLIC ARTWORKS

Jacob Dahlgren, *Early One Morning: Eternity Sculpture*
Swedish artist's squiggly pink 2019 sculpture in Kalasatama district is a fine example of playful constructivism

Risto Salonen, *Heijastuksia (Reflections)*
On Merihaka waterfront, this 1977 polished-aluminium and plate-glass sculpture reflects the surrounding ground, water and sky

Hannu Sirén, *Symboli (The Symbol)*
This 1985 minimalist steel ball, 3m (10ft) in diameter, faces Hakaniemi marketplace

Reijo Hukkanen, *Laulupuut (Pike's Song)*
Rising high in the square in front of Musiikkitalo (Helsinki Music Centre) since 2021, this 13m-high (43ft) steel sculpture of a singing pike is a showstopper

Kirsi Kaulanen, *Mare Mare (Sea, Sea)*
This sinuous sculpture in Loviseholm Park is a fantasy garden of plants and gnarled roots, laser-cut in stainless steel

Emma Jääskeläinen, *Put Put*
Striking shell-and-pearl sculpture, in the residential area of Herttoniemi, that draws the link to the sea

Eila Hiltunen, *Sibelius Monument*
Attention-grabbing sound wave in Sibelius Park that combines 600 soaring organ pipes in an ode to seminal Finnish composer Jean Sibelius (1865–1957)

Hannu Sirén, *Symboli (The Symbol)*
This 1985 minimalist steel ball, 3m (10ft) in diameter, faces Hakaniemi marketplace

Pekka Kauhanen, *National Memorial to the Winter War*
In front of the army headquarters, this 2017 sculpture of a giant, holey steel man contains 105 photographs of the Winter War

Above: *Kunsthalle Helsinki, housed in a building from 1928, with characteristics of Nordic Classicism;* ***Right:*** *Art and shadows inside the Ateneum Art Museum;* ***Opposite:*** *Jacob Dahlgren's Early One Morning, Eternity Sculpture.*

GLASGOW, SCOTLAND

Postindustrial glow-up

WHEN TO GO

The shoulder months (April–May and September–October) are perfect for sightseeing without the biggest crowds.

GETTING THERE

Fly in via Glasgow International Airport (GLA). Major US and European cities offer connecting flights through hubs such as London and Amsterdam.

It's pleasing to see how proud Glaswegians are of their hometown and its ongoing renaissance of urban cool. The Scottish city – its name in Gaelic roughly translates to 'grey-green hollow' or, colloquially, 'dear green place' – is more colourful than ever, with its brick-and-steel facades becoming homes and canvases for modern art.

Glasgow might not immediately come to mind as one of Europe's great art destinations, but in fact it's right up there with Paris and Rome – plus, its most fabulous venues are even free to visit. A legacy of Impressionism and realism is realised in charming rural Scottish landscapes, while portraits of everyday life – often with a focus on detail and texture – recall a simpler, bucolic side of Glasgow's 19th-century reputation as the 'Second City of the Empire' after London. Meanwhile, beautifully restored Art Nouveau buildings, flaunting intricate floral and geometric motifs, provide a vibrant counterpoint to gritty industrialism – a contrast that is entirely unique to Glasgow alone.

Best of all, the homegrown legacies of the Glasgow Boys and Scottish Colourists painters and of architect and designer Charles Rennie Mackintosh are testaments to the city's creativity, resilience and high-spirited nature.

***Right:** The stately neoclassical home of Glasgow's Gallery of Modern Art; **Opposite:** Kelvingrove Art Gallery's capacious Expression Court with The Heads by Sophy Cave.*

KELVINGROVE ART GALLERY & MUSEUM

The Kelvingrove has exhibitions from local legends such as the Glasgow Boys and the Scottish Colourists, but also international artists, from Monet to Matisse, with fine collections of French and Dutch Impressionist works, plus Italian Renaissance paintings to boot. Don't miss Salvador Dalí's *Christ of St John of the Cross*.

GALLERY OF MODERN ART (GoMA)

GoMA is a must-visit for its expansive collection showcasing Glasgow's bold, progressive side – plus, like Kelvingrove, it's also free admission. In a courtly neoclassical building, find notable works by Andy Warhol and David Hockney, as well as modern Scottish art spanning diverse media and styles.

Mackintosh House

Glasgow-born architect and designer **Charles Rennie Mackintosh** (1868–1928) was a leading darling of the Arts and Crafts movement's anti-response to Victorian-era industrialisation and mass production. Through the revival of traditional artisanship, emphasising hand-making and high-quality materials, Mackintosh blended Art Nouveau and modern sensibilities with his distinct style.

While there are many venues to discover Mackintosh's masterpieces across Glasgow, the **Mackintosh House** at the **Hunterian Art Gallery** is the quintessential example. It is a thoughtful reconstruction of Charles Rennie Mackintosh's Victorian end-of-terrace Glasgow home with his wife, designer and artist Margaret Macdonald. Demolished in the early 1960s, the house was remodelled and reassembled by architects, designers and historians, and opened to the public in 1981. The sequence of rooms exactly reflects the original, using natural light, clean lines and minimal ornamentation for a sculptural yet functional space.

Where the Mackintosh legacy really comes alive, though, are via interior furnishings, which all belonged to the Mackintoshes, and were made to their creative vision. Iconic pieces, from high-backed chairs to unusually shaped tables, blend form and function seamlessly. Meanwhile, in the ultra-white drawing room, beaten-silver panels and surface decorations of Celtic manuscript illuminations create an air of surreal elegance.

A·BOOK·OF·PARODIES

CORNWALL, ENGLAND

Cliffs and coves inspire modern art

WHEN TO GO
June, July or September, avoiding the busy school summer holidays.

GETTING THERE
Trains and buses connect London to St Ives.

With a dramatic landscape of wave-lashed cliffs and heather-clad moors, England's southwestern peninsula has attracted artists since JMW Turner painted his *St Michael's Mount* in the late 19th century. Following the extension of the Great Western Railway to West Cornwall in 1877, rugged Penwith Peninsula hosted a series of artistic groups, with the Newlyn School painting the Land's End area's soft light, maritime skies and fishing communities. See their work at Penzance's **Penlee House Gallery & Museum**, stay at Higher Faugan Parc, built for group founder Stanhope Forbes, and take classes at the namesake **Newlyn School of Art**.

Cornwall's association with creativity and alternative lifestyles – electronic musician Richard D James (aka Aphex Twin) grew up in Redruth, spy novelist John le Carré lived in St Buryan, and you're never far from a Celtic Cross pendant – reached its zenith with the St Ives School's landscape-inspired abstractions. Harbourside St Ives remains an art hub with its Tate and Barbara Hepworth museums, while the county's Gulf Stream–warmed gardens offer a holiday-perfect mix of culture and outdoorsy appeal. Follow garden paths to sculptures and galleries at **Tremenheere Sculpture Gardens**, the **Eden Project** and the **Lost Gardens of Heligan** – all members of the Great Gardens of Cornwall.

BARBARA HEPWORTH MUSEUM & SCULPTURE GARDEN

Yorkshire-born Dame Barbara Hepworth was one of the most important sculptors in 20th-century British art, creating abstract forms inspired by the Cornish landscape at her St Ives studio. The fisher's cottage where Hepworth lived and sculpted now houses a museum alongside her whitewashed workshop, while her enigmatic bronzes stand where she placed them in the wild garden.

TATE ST IVES

This seafront outpost of London's Tate galleries gives a sense of the vibrant artists' community that developed around Hepworth and her painter husband Ben Nicholson. The purpose-built building displays locally inspired artworks by Patrick Heron, Naum Gabo and Bridget Riley among others.

Right: *Tate St Ives entranceway;* ***Above:*** *The workshop at the Barbara Hepworth Museum and Sculpture Garden;* ***Opposite:*** *Fishing boats in St Ives' harbour.*

LONDON, ENGLAND

Cultural in the capital

WHEN TO GO
June, July or September, avoiding the busy school summer holidays; or in October for the Frieze art fairs.

GETTING THERE
London has two international airports, Heathrow (LHR) and Gatwick (LGW), and smaller airports at Stansted (STN), Luton (LTN) and London City (LCY).

The British capital is inarguably one of the world's great art cities, with more than 500 museums, galleries and cultural landmarks on either side of the River Thames. Londoners 'do the galleries' with as much relish as they hit the department stores and the Royal Parks – a cultural day here could mean touring East London's independent galleries, studios and collectives, experiencing an immersive art exhibition, or catching a Thames Clipper boat between the two Tate museums. Whether you're interested in discovering the next stars of the avant-garde, seeing a blockbuster retrospective, viewing the highlights of a Sotheby's auction, hunting down Banksy murals or contemplating some of the world's greatest fine-art collections, Soho and the South Bank will keep you busy.

An inspiring aspect of this cultural powerhouse is its heritage of artists who have lived, worked, trained and found inspiration on these streets. The most famous group of recent decades is the conceptual Young British Artists (YBAs), such as Damien Hirst and Tracey Emin, many of whom emerged from Goldsmiths college. But the story goes back further to pop artists, the Pre-Raphaelites, JMW Turner, William Blake and many more – the feeling of following a trail of culture-shaping individuals and movements is intoxicating.

TATE MODERN

The former Bankside Power Station is both an architectural marvel and a rich centre of modern and contemporary art, with 7827 sq metres (84,250 sq ft) of exhibition space. The vast Turbine Hall is a postindustrial cathedral which often hosts large-scale installations; children make a beeline for the Starr Foyer's Tate Draw digital sketchpads.

THE NATIONAL GALLERY

With its neoclassical pillars facing Nelson's Column on Trafalgar Sq, this 200-year-old public gallery houses more than 2000 artworks from the 13th century onwards, ranging from Jan van Eyck's *Arnolfini Portrait* (1434) to Vincent van Gogh's *Sunflowers* (1888). Highlights include the blockbuster exhibitions and the Sainsbury Wing's collection of early Renaissance art.

Left: *Tate Modern, set in a former power station on the Thames' South Bank;* ***Above:*** *The neoclassical National Gallery building on Trafalgar Sq;* ***Opposite:*** *Inside the National Portrait Gallery.*

Epiphone
BOAC

Museum houses

In a city where the baroque composer George Frideric Handel and rock legend Jimi Hendrix lived on the same Mayfair street, some 209 years apart, there are many former homes of creative giants to explore. In the world of visual arts, the early 19th-century home of the trailblazing painter of stormy British landscapes, JMW Turner, makes for a fascinating excursion to leafy southwest London. The Romantic artist designed Sandycombe Lodge (now known as **Turner's House**), located across the Thames from Richmond Park, and lived here with his father, enjoying this peaceful retreat from the London art world. A mix of period furniture, Turner etchings and digital installations evoke the 12 years he spent in the cottage, which was restored in 2016.

In nearby Holland Park, **Leighton House** was the lavish home and studio of Victorian painter, sculptor and aesthete Frederic, Lord Leighton. The Pre-Raphaelite associate's travels to Europe, North Africa and the Middle East inspired the ornately tiled Arab Hall and Narcissus Hall, while he worked in the glass-roofed Winter Studio during the darker months, and the Silk Room displays his collection of paintings by the likes of Sir John Everett Millais. With a combined ticket you can also visit the nearby home of Victorian *Punch* cartoonist Linley Sambourne.

LONDON LANDMARKS

The Shard
Architect Renzo Piano's skyscraper has a 72nd-floor open-air skydeck

Houses of Parliament
Big Ben clock tower dominates the 19th-century Palace of Westminster

St Paul's Cathedral
A vast dome crowns Sir Christopher Wren's baroque Anglican cathedral

The Gherkin
Architect Norman Foster's 41-floor pickle dominates the financial district

Barbican Centre
Brutalism finds its purest expression in the concrete ziggurat

Battersea Power Station
Its four chimneys grace the cover of Pink Floyd's *Animals*

The Walkie-Talkie
A garden tops the 40-floor 'handset' at 20 Fenchurch St

Buckingham Palace
Tours visit the State Rooms of the 775-room neoclassical palace

The Cheesegrater
The late Richard Rogers designed the wedge-shaped Leadenhall Building

Lloyd's building
Rogers' 1986 'inside-out building' was a trailblazer for contemporary architecture

Westminster Abbey
Glorious 13th-century-Gothic site of coronations and royal weddings

Tower of London
The capital's oldest intact building, begun by William the Conqueror

British Museum
Bloomsbury's stately trove of artefacts exemplifies the Greek Revival style

National Theatre
Architectural tours explore this brutalist masterpiece on the South Bank

Royal Albert Hall
Kensington's red-brick Victorian rotunda has hosted music's biggest names

Left: *An abundance of antiquity at Sir John Soane's Museum;* ***Below:*** *The soaring Great Court at the British Museum;* ***Opposite:*** *Street art on show at the Saatchi Gallery.*

CAPITAL GALLERIES

Tate Britain
The original Tate gallery displays 500 years of British masterpieces

National Portrait Gallery
A hub for portraiture, from bygone monarchs to contemporary photography

Saatchi Gallery
Advertising mogul Charles Saatchi founded this major contemporary art gallery

ICA (Institute of Contemporary Arts)
A go-to for cutting-edge art, cinema and performances in Westminster

V&A (Victoria & Albert Museum)
Enjoy 11km (7 miles) of galleries celebrating decorative arts, design and more

Young V&A
An inspiring cultural space for children in eastern Bethnal Green

Hayward Gallery
Long-running contemporary gallery in the concrete-clad Southbank Centre

Wallace Collection
A Georgian mansion brimming with 14th- to 19th-century fine art

Whitechapel Gallery
A platform for avant-garde artists from East London and beyond

Somerset House
A neoclassical complex on the Strand champions multidisciplinary contemporary culture

Courtauld Gallery
A significant collection of art from the Renaissance onwards

Kenwood House
Hampstead Heath's Georgian villa exhibits works by Rembrandt and others

Serpentine Galleries
Two contemporary art galleries alongside the eponymous Kensington Gardens lake

Royal Academy of Arts
Exhibits centuries of work by academicians at stately Burlington House, Piccadilly

Sir John Soane's Museum
The neoclassical architect's art-filled Holborn home evokes Regency London

Design Museum
The 10,000-sq-metre (107,639-sq-ft) Kensington home of London's leading contemporary design museum

AMSTERDAM, NETHERLANDS

All hail the golden era

WHEN TO GO

Summer is Amsterdam's peak tourist season, but art buffs will love winter's shortened queues and less-crowded museums (many open on public holidays).

GETTING THERE

Flying into Amsterdam's Schiphol Airport (AMS) is easy – it's the world's third-busiest for international passengers.

Amsterdam has the Dutch Masters to thank for its reputation as one of the world's greatest, bucket-list art destinations. During the 17th century, Golden Age painters such as Johannes Vermeer, Frans Hals and Rembrandt brushed up a storm, rolling in commissions from a new, bourgeois society of merchants and shopkeepers. Money was no object in beautifying homes and workplaces, resulting in the abundance of fine art adorning the 'Dam today.

Masters' subjects were incredibly diverse. Works are mainly characterised by intricate detail, realism, and depictions of everyday life from the era. There's portraiture of wealthy patrons, of course, but also stirring countryside and maritime landscapes as well as intimate still-life compositions of domestic life – always rife with symbolism to ponder.

The Golden Ages may get the highest glory, but Amsterdam's contemporary art scene leaves much to rave about too, especially in the historic marine industrial area of Amsterdam Noord: former shipyard buildings such as the **NDSM-Werf** and **Kunststad** here are havens for showcasing progressive, emerging young artists. The area's brick facades are an ever-changing open-air gallery of sprayed-on murals, and lead up to **STRAAT**, an incredible street-art and graffiti museum where you can watch artists at work.

RIJKSMUSEUM

Behold – this is one of the world's most illustrious (and most visited) art museums. Beyond the Rijksmuseum's grand archway entrance, explore labyrinthine galleries of of some 8000 artworks. The Rijks (pronounced 'rikes') is the epicentre for discovering the Dutch Masters, from Vermeer to Van Gogh – Rembrandt's *The Night Watch* (1642) is the museum's superstar, though Van Gogh's *Self-Portrait* (1887) also shouldn't be missed.

VAN GOGH MUSEUM

Van Gogh's artworks are dispersed across museums worldwide, but here is the largest collection of all – 200 paintings and 500 drawings – as well as works from his contemporaries, such as Gauguin, Toulouse-Lautrec and Monet. Exhibits chronicle his life and artistic evolution, from sombre Dutch farm days to sunny, blissful France.

Above: *Gathering in front of Rembrandt's The Night Watch at the Rijksmuseum;* ***Opposite:*** *Graffiti and street art take centre stage at STRAAT.*

Wereldmuseum Amsterdam

Renamed from the Tropenmuseum in 2023, the Wereldmuseum – an ethnographic museum on world cultures – offers an important artistic counterpoint to Amsterdam's showcases of Dutch Masters works.

During the 17th century, colonisation and trade via overseas territories helped make the Dutch empire the most prosperous nation in Europe – and ultimately financed Golden Age artworks and scientific developments through rising bourgeois buying power. The Wereldmuseum – first opened in 1864 in Haarlem as the Colonial Museum – actively confronts the Netherlands' past, encouraging important discussions on the effect of colonial histories on current societies. Displays are often centred around cultural artefacts, though these can often be taken in through an artistic lens too – from showcases of historical photographs and temporary exhibitions on textiles, folk costumes or traditional clothing to historical archives of the museum's own colonial origins. Meanwhile, the permanent collection, Things That Matter, focuses on identity and themes that connect people and places from all over the globe.

Insights into the past's unfair balance of power between Europeans and non-Europeans, and the procurement of cultural artefacts and artwork through colonial oppression or otherwise – presented in vibrant, imaginative ways through much multimedia – make the museum an engaging visit for adults and little ones alike.

WERELDMUSEUM

COLOGNE, GERMANY

Street art and modernist masterpieces on the Rhine

WHEN TO GO

In early November for Museum Night, when galleries open late, and the Art Cologne fair.

GETTING THERE

The city is well connected to Cologne Bonn (CGN), Düsseldorf (DUS) and Frankfurt (FRA) airports.

Germany's western city of Cologne (Köln) is best known for its vast Gothic cathedral, which miraculously survived the WWII bombs that flattened the area around its 157m-high (515ft) twin spires. Postwar reconstruction has given the Rhineland cultural centre a vibrant contemporary spirit, with young people crowding *biergartens*, and street-art tours discovering the murals of Ehrenfeld and the Belgian Quarter. There are more than 100 museums for a million locals, including the design-focused **Museum für Angewandte Kunst** (Museum of Applied Arts), **Kolumba's Art Museum of the Archdiocese of Cologne**, and those covering the region's chocolate- and cologne-making heritage.

Beethoven may have come from rival Bonn, but Cologne produced Nico, the Andy Warhol acolyte and husky-voiced singer for Lou Reed's Velvet Underground. Check out this heritage at the blockbuster Museum Ludwig, displaying chocolate-magnate Peter Ludwig's collection of pop art. He also donated an important medieval and modern-art collection to his home town of Aachen, making the nearby spa city worth a visit for its **Suermondt-Ludwig Museum** and **Ludwig Forum for International Art**. Don't miss the 9th-century emperor Charlemagne's gilded shrine in Aachen Cathedral and, if you need a book for the train from Cologne, browse the Taschen Store for a tome by the city's luxury art publisher.

Right: *Museum Ludwig, Cologne's cathedral to modern and contemporary art;* ***Opposite:*** *Kolumba combines the ruins of a Gothic church with modern architecture.*

MUSEUM LUDWIG

This sprawling '80s monolith between Cologne Cathedral and the Rhine houses one of Europe's most impressive modern-art collections, assembled by Peter and Irene Ludwig. The wide-ranging display includes the continent's most extensive pop-art collection, the world's third-largest Picasso collection, and significant German Expressionism and photography sections.

KÄTHE KOLLWITZ MUSEUM KÖLN

The Neumarkt Passage shopping arcade is an unassuming setting for this comprehensive collection of more than 300 drawings and 550-plus prints alongside posters and sculptures by the influential expressionist Käthe Kollwitz. Her raw etchings and woodcuts offer heart-wrenchingly honest depictions of poor and downtrodden Berliners from the 1890s to the 1940s.

BERLIN, GERMANY

Urban art playground

WHEN TO GO

Summer is the best time to explore and even picnic against endless open-air murals.

GETTING THERE

Fly into Berlin (BER) via European hubs such as Amsterdam and London (or direct from New York City).

In Berlin, underground culture reigns supreme, and no other European city is as impassioned about pushing artistic freedom to the outer limits. Creative expression in the German capital prizes nonconformism, progressiveness – and being just a little weird and offbeat.

Of course, a legacy of open-mindedness has emerged from the oppressive experiences of WWII and the Cold War. The fall of the Berlin Wall in 1989 galvanised the arts scene, which today thrives on subcultural impulses, electronic music and gritty urban transformation. Yes, Berlin is home to polished gallery elegance, (the world-class, UNESCO-recognised **Museum Island** is the premiere example), but the city's street-art murals and esoteric collections in squats, derelict factories and gloomy bunkers? That's where art buffs are destined to truly fall in love.

Plus, club culture goes hand-in-hand with the creative circuit. Graffiti, performance art and DIY installations play a big part in Berlin nightlife and directly contribute to creating the over-the-top hedonistic escapism of its famous techno raves and sex-positive parties.

Overall, Berlin's scene can only be described as the epitome of diverse and eclectic. No wonder multidisciplinary, multicultural artists flock here in droves to create and be inspired.

EAST SIDE GALLERY

You might know it better as the Berlin Wall's longest still-existing stretch. Officially known as the East Side Gallery, this open-air art showcase – the world's longest – is an urban spectacle. Stroll the nearly 1.6km-long (1 mile) stretch where some 100 murals from international artists immortalise postwar optimism and unity, from the famous *Fraternal Kiss* to Thierry Noir's cartoons.

URBAN NATION

It's no surprise that the world's first urban contemporary art museum is located in graffitied-up Berlin. Urban Nation's walls, once housing a former print shop, now contain over 100 exhibits, spanning stencils to zines and sculpture. Even the facade is a constantly reinvented canvas for travelling artists.

Right: *Graffiti art in Berlin's nightlife-focused Friedrichshain district;* ***Above:*** *The East Side Gallery on the longest intact stretch of the Berlin Wall;* ***Opposite:*** *Urban Nation, Berlin's homage to urban contemporary art.*

Sammlung Boros (Boros Collection)

Look out for the unsightly concrete block against Mitte's grand historic architecture – it's a war bunker and, unsuspectingly, houses Berlin's coolest privately-owned art collection. The Boros Collection is a labyrinthine, 3000-sq-metre (32,292-sq-ft) space where rooms have spanned the who's who of contemporary artists, including Ai Weiwei, Wolfgang Tillmans and Damien Hirst.

Beyond a mighty exciting collection, the bunker high-rise tells a fascinating story about Berlin. It was constructed in 1942 as a Nazi air-raid shelter, with nearly indestructible walls aimed at protecting up to 3000 civilians. During the Cold War, the space was repurposed as an East German storage facility for textiles and, later, for tropical fruit imported from Cuba (earning it the nickname 'Banana Bunker'). Following German reunification, it became a symbol for creativity and self-expression in Berlin's underground culture, hosting wild techno raves and fetish parties.

Since 2008, the Boros has displayed 500-plus pieces on its lower levels – ranging across various media from sculptures to spatial installations, and light and performance works. Meanwhile, the owner – a well-known advertising guru and art collector – lives with his family upstairs.

Admission is considered rather exclusive: it's only available via guided tours held four days a week. Make sure to prebook at least a few weeks in advance.

ART MUSEUMS

Bode-Museum
Era-spanning European sculptures and rare Byzantine art

Alte Nationalgalerie
The Old National Gallery is a grandiose temple to European art: Gothic, Romantic and onwards

Hamburger Bahnhof – Nationalgalerie der Gegenwart
Berlin's premier modern-art gallery in a former railway station

Berlinische Galerie
Deutsch modern galore, from Dada to New Objectivity and Eastern avant-garde

Gemäldegalerie
Around 1500 paintings spanning 13th- to 18th-century European art

Neue Nationalgalerie
Twentieth-century rock stars, from Cubism to Surrealism and Bauhaus

C/O Berlin
Beloved photography centre showing internationally acclaimed artists and aspiring talents

Fotografiska Berlin
Local post of the world-famous photo museum in a factory of cool

Humboldt Forum
'Germany's British Museum' – don't miss its Museum of Asian Art

Museum of Photography
Snaps since the 19th century, including a permanent Helmut Newton exhibition

Gropius Bau
Where the worlds flashiest modern-art exhibits show in Berlin

Above: *Christian KERA Hinz's Pool Painting, at the Hošek Contemporary;* ***Middle:*** *Berlin's venerable Bode-Museum on Museum Island;* ***Opposite:*** *Photography is the star at C/O Berlin.*

ALTERNATIVE (& UNEXPECTED) ART VENUES

RAW-Gelände
A graffiti-covered maze of industrial warehouses turned entertainment venues

Berghain/Panorama Bar
World-famous techno club; periodically programmes exhibits too

Kunstraum Kreuzberg/Bethanien
Peek into artists' ateliers in a stately former hospital (and squat)

KW Institute for Contemporary Art
'Always out-there and never permanent' is the exhibition mantra here

Freiraum in der Box
Radical, socio-political art displayed in a former stables

Hošek Contemporary
Climb aboard a floating gallery on a Spree River barge

SomoS Arts
Up-and-coming artists in residence pushing against the mainstream

The Feuerle Collection
Elusive exhibits of Asian antiques and art in a bunker

König Galerie
Brutalist church space showcasing well-curated works by next-gen artists

Studio Olafur Eliasson
World-famous installation studio, sometimes open for workshops and events

Anomalie Art Club
Rave nightclub where dance floors are framed by pop-up exhibitions

SLOVAKIA

BRATISLAVA,

Unsung capital, outsize art scene

WHEN TO GO
Spring and summer bring sunny weather and artistic and musical festivals. Don't miss the Coronation Days.

GETTING THERE
Budget flights to Bratislava Airport (BTS) abound. Night-jet sleeper trains run from Brussels to Vienna, an hour from Bratislava by bus/train.

Bratislava is perched at the meeting point of Slovakia, Austria and Hungary, and this cross-border cocktail influences everything from the culinary scene to the arts. In a city that has weathered centuries of changing borders, local creatives are fuelled to explore themes of language, identity and the passage of time.

But art and pageantry were part of Bratislava's DNA long before Slovakia became a sovereign state in 1993. This was the coronation city of the Hungarian Kingdom for three centuries, during which aristocrats shipped in artists from around Europe to fill their palaces with sculptures, mosaics and murals. Many of these regal residences, like **Pálffy Palace**, can be visited today – but you can feel Bratislava's artistic pulse almost anywhere.

There's the **Old Town**, where pastel colours backdrop Renaissance fountains and sculptures of modern-day eccentrics (look down on Panská to see *Čumil*, Viktor Hulík's rascally sewer-worker peeping from a maintenance hole). Dystopian aesthetics slice through the city in constructions like the **UFO Building** – a reminder of Bratislava's austere, state-regulated '70s. Then there's the topsy-turvy **Slovak Radio Building**, which locals proudly tell you is one of the world's ugliest. If art is made memorable by contradiction and grit, then Bratislava is the grandest canvas.

DANUBIANA MEULENSTEEN ART MUSEUM

Shaped like a warship and buttressed with rainbow-bright sculptures, this modern-art gallery juts into the Danube River. Inside is a collection of experimental 20th- and 21st-century European art, particularly by Czech and Slovak artists – from Erik Šille's vivid acrylics to saintly visions by Dorota Sadovská. Enormous windows expose the Danube's waters, like nature is part of the show.

SLOVAK NATIONAL GALLERY (SNG)

Take a lavish baroque residence, add a dash of brutalism, then shake it up with an award-winning 2023 makeover. Diverse architectural styles set the tone for the SNG's mix of old and new art, and confronting exhibitions grapple with themes like conflict and national identity.

Above: *Inside the Slovak National Gallery (SNG);* ***Opposite:*** *Peter Pollág's Danube Wings, one of 60 sculptures in the Danubiana Meulensteen grounds;* ***Next spread:*** *The bold brutalist extension of the SNG's Esterházy Palace building.*

Klimt: rebel with a cause

Any talk of that most famous of Viennese painters, Gustav Klimt (1862–1918), is bound to zoom in on sensational works like *The Kiss* (1907) and biblical *Judith* (1901), which hang in all their gold-leaf brilliance in the lavish galleries of the **Upper Belvedere Palace**.

But to truly get a handle on Klimt, you need to reach back further to the genesis of the Wiener Secession (Vienna Secession) movement. In 1897, Vienna was a city artistically on the move. Tired of the rigid rules and neoclassical style of the Akademie der Bildenden Künste (Academy of Fine Arts), a group of daring, rebellious artists and architects decided to swim away from the mainstream, among them Klimt, Otto Wagner, Joseph Maria Olbrich and Josef Hoffman. In 1898, Olbrich designed the **Secession Hall**, a masterpiece blending functionality and modernism, nicknamed the 'Golden Cabbage' for its dome of intertwining golden vines. In 1902, the hall formed the backdrop for their 14th exhibition, devoted to Beethoven. Visit the basement and you'll be mesmerised by the work Klimt created to mark the occasion: the 34m-long (112ft) *Beethoven Frieze,* an ode to Beethoven's joyous 9th Symphony.

LAUSANNE, SWITZERLAND

Lake Geneva's contemporary-arts hub

For a medium-sized city, Lausanne offers a surprisingly rich cultural life, with museums, galleries, festivals and other events that animate its arts scene. This city of 150,000 in Switzerland's Francophone region rises above Lake Geneva, with scenic pathways and beaches along the lakeshore, and an urban core built into the hills higher up. (A short, steep metro line connects the lakefront with the centre.) The headquarters of the International Olympic Committee (IOC) since 1915, Lausanne is home to the Olympic Museum, which shares stories of the Olympic Games past and present. A recently opened arts district known as **Plateforme 10** has created a hub for several of the region's art museums.

If you prefer to explore art while you wander, check out *Art en Ville* (Art in the City), a Lausanne-produced guide that leads you to more than 80 public classical and contemporary artworks, plus museums and cafes. While Lausanne hosts cultural festivals throughout the year, try to visit in July for the annual **Festival de la Cité**, a lively week of free concerts, circus shows, dance and other performances.

WHEN TO GO

Visit April through October for best weather, July through September for outdoor arts and music festivals.

GETTING THERE

Reach Lausanne on direct trains from airports in Geneva (GVA; 45–60 minutes) or Zurich (ZRH; 2½ hours) and from most other Swiss cities.

Below: *Creative lighting bathes Lausanne's Cathédrale de Notre Dame in colour;* ***Left:*** *Outsider art at Collection de l'Art Brut.*

PLATEFORME 10

Built on the site of former railway repair yards opposite Lausanne's central train station, the city's newest arts district includes three contemporary museums: Musée Cantonal des Beaux-Arts, the region's fine-arts museum; mudac, the Museum of Contemporary Design and Applied Arts; and Photo Elysée, a photography gallery.

LA COLLECTION DE L'ART BRUT

This gallery of 'outsider art' features works by self-taught artists, many of whom are dealing with psychiatric issues or with other mental or physical challenges. Set in the 18th-century Château de Beaulieu, the museum has a permanent collection of 700 works by 60 creators, which it shows in rotating exhibits.

Old made new: reinventing artful spaces

In a city with a history stretching back millennia, Lausanners have become experts at reinvention, transforming heritage structures into museums, galleries and restaurants. While the Plateforme 10 arts district may be the most recent example, many other historic spaces have been repurposed.

The **Fondation de l'Hermitage**, a visual-arts museum high above the city centre, was once the summer estate of the wealthy Bugnion family, who constructed their home in the mid-1850s, eventually donating the property to the city. Since the 1980s, it has hosted regular exhibitions, many focusing on artists of French-speaking Switzerland.

A district of industrial warehouses was revamped to create the **Flon**, a hip pedestrian hub of cafes, galleries and shops, plus clubs that buzz until late. A row of 'garages', once workshops of local craftspeople, house tiny boutiques and storefront art spaces.

The walls of **Lausanne Cathedral**, a Gothic church dating to the 1200s, are often used for art shows. Bookend your art wanderings with meals in restaurants Brasserie de Montbenon, in a grand 1908 manor with one of the city's most beautiful terraces; or Café de Grancy, a 19th-century building transformed into a contemporary bistro. Because in Lausanne, 'old' is artfully new.

PARIS, FRANCE

Premier art capital

WHEN TO GO

Paris is fantastic year-round. Summer can be busy and expensive. During August many Parisians leave and some restaurants close.

GETTING THERE

Fly into either Orly (ORY) or Charles de Gaulle (CGD), or take trains across France and Europe to one of numerous stations.

Paris is one of the world's great art cities, and its priceless treasures are showcased in palatial museums, contemporary galleries and innovative multimedia spaces. With a skyline marked by the Eiffel Tower, Arc de Triomphe and Notre Dame, just looking around is a feast, while stepping inside Sainte-Chapelle reveals stunning stained glass.

And where else can you revel in a museum dedicated to sculptor-painter-engraver Auguste Rodin? His entire collection is resplendent in his former workshop and showroom, the beautiful 1730 **Hôtel Biron**, and its rose-filled garden. Where else can you see the world's largest collection of works by Impressionist painter Claude Monet (1840–1926) – at **Musée Marmottan Monet**?

It wouldn't be Paris without fashion. Thrillingly creative **Musée Yves Saint Laurent Paris** is right near its equal, **La Galerie Dior**. Perfectly curated special exhibits fill fashion museum **Palais Galliera**.

In the streets, art is all around you, from loose graffiti to murals covering entire high-rises. Paris' gardens are art-filled, too – **Jardin du Luxembourg** alone has over 100 sculptures. And creativity greets you even in death: browse elaborate tombs at **Cimetière du Père Lachaise** and ossuaries in **Les Catacombes**. And that's without touching on day-trips to Versailles and Giverny.

Right: *Sculptures and visitors in the Rodin Museum garden;* ***Opposite:*** *Pan playing his flute in the colorful Jardin du Luxembourg.*

MUSÉE DU LOUVRE

You could spend weeks here and never really see it all. Pick your mood, head into the former royal palace, and you will find something to satisfy, whether ancient Greek artefacts, lush-toned Renaissance paintings or Impressionist masterpieces. Just lounging by its fountains as the sun sets golden over the intricate facades and shining pyramid is exalting.

ATELIER BRANCUSI

With its arts-for-all philosophy, the Centre Pompidou offers the inspiring Constantin Brâncuși studio free of charge. The faithful recreation of the sculptor's final studio showcases his striking geometric works in brilliant juxtaposition. Exit from its garden courtyard to the Pompidou's plaza and catch music performances and urban art gatherings.

FACE AU VIDE

Sustainable art incubators

Beyond the classic Parisian museums and galleries, alternative arts-and-music hubs are springing up all around the city. Combining contemporary art spaces with live music, they feature interesting cafes, markets or shops, often with an emphasis on sustainability.

In the 19th arrondissement, the funeral parlour turned city-funded alternative art space **Le 104** supports young artists, and a wander through reveals breakdancers, edgy art installations and singers rehearsing. Check the schedule for a robust slate of art expositions, theatre, concerts and more. Grab a bite at its airy restaurant–bar, retro cafe or pizza truck.

POUSH, the city's biggest contemporary art incubator, fills a repurposed factory in Aubervilliers. It's huge, so there's always a thought-provoking array of shows, and it sponsors events off-site, too. Plus, it hosts La Station, a platform for emerging musical artists.

Nearby, seek out the immensely popular urban project **La Cité Fertile**, set in a former freight-train station. Food, drinks and recreation, from petanque to meditation, combine with sustainable-food markets, music and art installations.

An abandoned Petite Ceinture train station has been repurposed as an eco-hub called **La Recyclerie**. It's got an urban farm along the old railway line supplying its mostly vegetarian cafe-canteen, and runs upcycling workshops, flea markets (for the art sleuth) and other events.

PARIS ART MUSEUMS

Musée D'Orsay
Fabulous former railway station with a vital collection of Impressionists and Post-Impressionists

Musée National du Moyen Âge (Musée de Cluny)
Middle Ages masterpieces in the Latin Quarter's magnificent Hôtel de Cluny

Musée du Luxembourg
Excellent temporary art exhibitions amid the Jardin du Luxembourg

Centre Pompidou
Radical architecture meets cutting-edge exhibitions, hands-on workshops and events

Musée de l'Orangerie & Jeu de Palme
Jardin des Tuileries museums with Monet's *Water Lilies* and innovative photography

MAD (Musée des Arts Décoratifs)
Arts and design repository, with fantastic Art Nouveau and Art Deco pieces

Musée Jacquemart-André
Opulent residence with Titian, Botticelli and Rembrandt alongside antiquities

Musée du Quai Branly
World art spans Oceania and Asia to Africa and the Americas

Musée Picasso
Over 5000 Picassos rotate through the mid-17th-century Hôtel Salé

L'Atelier des Lumières
Paris' first digital-art museum: dazzling light projections in an 1835 foundry

l'Institut du Monde Arabe
The Institute of the Arab World has excellent rotating shows in a Jean Nouvel–designed building on the Seine

Musée des Arts Forains
Remarkable collection of enchanting fairground and carnival artefacts

Musée Zadkine
Former home and atelier of Russian-born sculptor Ossip Zadkine

Musée National Eugène Delacroix
Romantic artist's home and studio contains his oil paintings, watercolours and pastels

PUBLIC ART

Invader tiles
Ubiquitous tiled Space Invaders–inspired creations marking street corners

Stravinsky Fountain
Niki de Saint Phalle and Jean Tinguely's 16 playful animated sculptures

Pont Neuf
Paris' oldest bridge, adorned with 381 *mascarons* (grotesque figures)

Montparnasse's Blvd Vincent Auriol murals
Thirty monumental murals by the Faile collective, Shepard Fairey, Conor Harrington and others

Palais Royal columns
Daniel Buren's zebra-striped courtyard columns

Jardins des Tuileries & du Luxembourg
Sculptures from the 19th and early 20th centuries. Tuileries also has contemporary works

Art 42
Post-graffiti and street art at this 'anti-museum' includes Swoon and Miss Van

La Défense
Business district with dozens of pieces by artists such as Miró and Calder

Musée de la Sculpture en Plein Air
Over 50 late-20th-century sculptures along quai St-Bernard

Fédéric Baron and Claire Kito, *Le mur des je t'aime*
Selfie central: Montmartre's 'I Love You' wall speaks the language of love in enamel tiles

Metro station entrances
Hector Guimard's signature Art Nouveau entrances, such as Porte Dauphine

L'Aerosol
Street art in a former SNCF freight railway station, from Mr Chat to Banksy

Rue Oberkampf murals
Seek out Le MUR, overseen by an arts collective

La Villette canal basin
Stroll Rue de l'Ourcq to watch murals and graffiti unfurl

Galerie Itinerrance
Thirteenth arrondissement graffiti and street-art gallery

Fresh Street Art Paris
Want guidance? Get the low-down on a street-art tour

Clockwise from top left: *Keep eyes peeled for Paris' street-corner Space Invaders tiles; L'Atelier des Lumières, shining a light on digital art; The main gallery at Musée D'Orsay; Shepard Fairey's Liberté, Egalité, Fraternité mural on Blvd Vincent.*

1er ARRt
RUE
BERGER

AVÉ CÉSAR!

LIBERTE EGALITE

PROVENCE, FRANCE

Sun-kissed inspiration in the footsteps of Cézanne, Van Gogh and Picasso

WHEN TO GO
Visit Provence year-round; its art sights remain open. Summer blooms, but is crowded and expensive. Spring and autumn are a happy compromise.

GETTING THERE
Fly to Nice (NCE) or Marseille (MRS), or take a train (TGV) from Paris.

From the Palais de Papes in Avignon and its Renaissance-art-abundant **Musée du Petit Palais** to the French Riviera, the southern French region of Provence inspired dozens of artists to come, paint and settle.

In St-Tropez pointillism took off with Georges Seurat and was then picked up by his pupil Paul Signac, all on display at the **Musée de l'Annonciade**. Pierre-Auguste Renoir painted out his last Impressionist days in a villa, now **Musée Renoir**, in Cagnes-sur-Mer. He adored Nice, as did Marc Chagall, Henri Matisse and Pablo Picasso, perfect today for glorious architecture and its world-class museums of their work.

Picasso discovered the medieval village Vieux Mougins in 1935 and lived there from 1961 until his death. Antibes, on the sparkling Mediterranean, was another of his favourite spots – visit the **Musée Picasso** there.

Paul Cézanne is particularly celebrated for his Post-Impressionist still-lifes and landscapes done in Aix-en-Provence. Vincent van Gogh loved Arles and the Camargue; follow in his footsteps when walking around Arles, where both he and Paul Gauguin painted, and visit the **Fondation Vincent Van Gogh**. He also created many much-loved paintings in the Les Alpilles region while at the sanatorium **Monastère St-Paul de Mausole**, outside Saint-Rémy-de-Provence.

MONASTÈRE ST-PAUL DE MAUSOLE, SAINT-RÉMY-DE-PROVENCE

Vincent van Gogh admitted himself into this monastery-turned-asylum in 1889, introducing one of the most prolific periods of his life. He made over 150 drawings and as many paintings while living in a tiny room alongside a Romanesque cloister. Plants he painted are still grown here today.

MUSÉE PICASSO, ANTIBES

Pablo Picasso featured the town of Antibes, with its 16th-century ramparts and boat-lined port, in his paintings, and he himself said, 'If you want to see the Picassos from Antibes, you have to see them in Antibes.' Visit the 14th-century Château Grimaldi, Picasso's studio, where lithographs, paintings, drawings and ceramics show his versatility and curiosity.

Above: *Musée Picasso in the Château Grimaldi, Antibes;* ***Opposite:*** *Van Gogh produced hundreds of paintings and drawings during his stay at the Monastère St-Paul de Mausole, Saint-Rémy-de-Provence.*

In the footsteps of Cézanne, Aix-en-Provence

In Aix, follow the **Circuit de Cézanne** (Cézanne Trail), marked by bronze plaques, to see where Paul Cézanne lived, studied, painted, ate and drank. Then make your way to the **Atelier Cézanne**, his last studio, which is preserved in great verisimilitude. He worked here from 1902 until his death four years later, but though the studio is inspiring, and home to periodic exhibitions, none of Cézanne's works actually hang there. See actual paintings at the **Musée Granet**, alongside pieces by Matisse, Picasso, Léger, Klee, Monet and Van Gogh.

You can stand in other places where Cézanne painted and see them much as he did. **Terrain des Peintres**, near the Atelier, is a terraced garden from where he painted the silvery ridge of Montagne Ste-Victoire (over 80 renditions of it).

In 1859 Cézanne's father bought **Bastide du Jas de Bouffan**, an 18th-century country manor west of Aix where Cézanne painted furiously, producing 36 oils and 17 watercolours depicting the house, chestnut-tree avenue, garden and farm.

It's also well worth a trip to the **Carrières de Bibémus**, east of Aix, where Cézanne painted 27 works in 1895. Today you can tour the ochre quarry through the evocative burnt-orange rocks that Cézanne captured so vividly on canvas.

BARCELONA, SPAIN

Catalonia's crown jewel

WHEN TO GO
Late autumn (October–November) promises less-crowded streets, cooler temperatures and better fares.

GETTING THERE
Barcelona's El Prat Airport (BCN) serves cities worldwide. High-speed Renfe trains connect Sants Station to the rest of Spain, and Eurail services run from around Europe.

The tiled ceilings of El Prat's Terminal 1 *Sky Center*, by Catalan architect Ricardo Bofill, vie for attention with Terminal 2's massive mural by native son Joan Miró – arranged in serpentine, multicoloured ceramic – and hint to the visitor that they are entering a city touched by genius.

What is in the salty air of this port city that has given us Miró, Antoni Gaudí and Pablo Picasso? The spiritual and administrative heart of Catalonia, a world apart from Spain, Barcelona has fostered the nation's – and the world's – most influential and famous creators. It served as inspiration to an adolescent Picasso and Miró, who studied at the same Academy, as well as to budding cellist Pablo Casals.

Choose from museums dedicated to Picasso and Miró (and the bars they used to hang out in); spectacular buildings such as the sparkling **Palau de la Música Catalana**, and the incomparable residences and public spaces envisioned by native son Gaudí; or perhaps a one-hour side trip west to Figueres, birthplace of Salvador Dalí and home to his **Teatre-Museu Dalí**.

From the Barri Gòtic's labyrinthian cobblestone walkways to the surreal gardens of **Park Güell**, pedestrian-friendly BCN unveils itself at every turn to the appreciative eye.

LA SAGRADA FAMÍLIA

Gaudí, a devout Catholic, fittingly dubbed this shrine 'sacred'. Exotic pelicans and monkeys are carved into the church's entranceway; extraordinary stained-glass windows reach to the heavens and flood the interior with a kaleidoscope of colour. Amazingly, Mass takes place among the masses, and you can still find a quiet nook to meditate. Unfinished when Gaudí died in 1926, it remains in perpetual construction.

PARK GÜELL

Park Güell combines acres of Mediterranean gardens with the mad mosaic that was the mind of Gaudí. This former vineyard and olive grove is now a UNESCO World Heritage Site and, at 17 hectares (42 acres), a crucial green space for the city.

Right: *Gaudí mosaics at Park Güell;* ***Above:*** *Domènech i Montaner's Palau de la Música Catalana, with its spectacular stained-glass ceiling;* ***Opposite:*** *Gaudí's Sagrada Família, still a work in progress.*

Museu Picasso: kind of blue

Five stone medieval *paluas* (palazzos) on Carrer Montcada comprising Museu Picasso convey the weight of the artist's connection with place. When planning a museum with his friend Sabartés, Picasso suggested Barcelona. Born in Málaga and having lived most of his adult life in France, he nonetheless considered the city his spiritual home – the place where he attended art school, had his first exhibition, and made lifelong friends in the artistic community.

Jaume Sabartés with Pince-Nez (1901) is typical of his Blue Period portraits, and once hung at Barcelona's Els Quatre Gats cafe. *Blanquita Suarez*, from 1917, shows a more engaged, perhaps happier Picasso reflecting a fellow artist at work.

Visions of turn-of-the-century Barcelona abound: its balconies, cathedrals and seascapes; marvellous Montjuïc. *Barcelona Rooftops* (1902) are tinged in azure. A 'virtual tour' of Spain can be taken as well, with depictions of Málaga, Valencia and more.

Visitors can trace Picasso's artistic development and the breadth of his work (nearly 4000 pieces). Ceramics, engraving and painting comprise three pillars of the permanent collection; while most of the paintings date no later than 1917, the important *Meninas* series from 1957 appears in full. A charming film of the artist at home in Cannes runs in one of the salons.

GAUDI & THE THEATRE CROWD

Palau Güell
Another collaboration between Gaudí and his wealthy patron, this is secreted away on Las Ramblas and also a UNESCO World Heritage Site

Gran Teatre del Liceu
A classic 2000-seat theatre on Las Ramblas, a replica of the 1847 original

Casa Batlló
Another Gaudí masterwork: each oak door a wonder; mask-shaped balconies; and a dragon's-spine rooftop peopled with quartets of chimney-stacks

Casa Milà
Just up Pasaje de Gracia from Battló, 'La Pedrera' indeed resembles a stone quarry. Chiselled ceramic-and-cement warriors protect Barcelona's most memorable 360-degree view, while the attic's 270 arches make one feel in the belly of Jonah's epochal whale

Casa Vicens
Gaudí's first commission, a template for all to follow, includes a luscious garden filled with palms (mirroring the wrought-iron gate), magnolias and roses. Indoor highlights include Gaudí-designed wood furniture and papier-mâché tiles

Teatre Nacional de Catalunya
Ricardo Bofill's modernist structure rivals its musical and theatrical presentations as a work of art itself

Collegi d'Arquitectes de Catalunya
The friezes are generated from drawings by Picasso; the murals inside are by him as well

BARS, CAFES, MUSEUMS & PUBLIC ART

Bar Marsella
A dusty joint where Picasso got his drink (absinthe) on

Fundació Miró
A glass-and-concrete wonder in Parc Montjuïc, 184m (604ft) above the city and surrounded by botanical gardens, a castle and a magical fountain

Els Quatre Gats
'The Four Cats' was a haunt of Picasso and his modernist pals, and site of his first public show

Fernando Botero, *Gato (Cat)*
Colombia's noted celebrator of all things big created this huge bronze feline on the Rambla del Raval

Museu Nacional d'Art de Catalunya
Montjuïc gem, comprising modernist works and 300-plus Renaissance and baroque pieces by Rubens, El Greco, Cranach and more

Muse d'Art Contemporani de Barcelona (MACBA)
This funky white 'pearl' designed by American architect Richard Meier comprises three galleries with art from the 1940s and later

Teatre-Museu Dalí, Figueres
The uniquely glass-domed surrealist collection on the coast is well worth the hour's train trip from Barcelona

Above: *The serpentine lines of Gaudí's Casa Batlló;* ***Right:*** *Figueres' Teatre-Museu Dalí, designed by the artist himself;* ***Opposite:*** *The chimneys of Gaudí's Casa Milà, aka La Pedrera.*

MALLORCA, SPAIN

Miró's dream-island home

WHEN TO GO

Palma and Sóller are great year-round. Warm months are best for the rest of the island.

GETTING THERE

Fly into Mallorca Airport (PMI) or take a ferry. Cala Major is a short bus ride from central Palma. Get to Sóller on the vintage train.

A short stroll around Palma quickly illustrates how Mallorca has been a place of artistic and architectural inspiration for centuries. Step into the magnificent cathedral, **La Seu**, rising above the harbour and the ancient sienna-toned city walls, and you'll encounter shimmering stained glass (including the largest rose window in Europe) alongside a fantastical baldachin by Antoni Gaudí, and a psychedelic-feeling chapel by local legend Miquel Barceló. Other art-encrusted churches carpet the city.

Museums in grand palaces – **Museu Fundación Juan March**, **Es Baluard** and **Fundación Bartolomé March** – enliven both eyes and minds with thought-proving work spanning modern and contemporary art and sculpture. They pair with excellent exhibitions in Palma's edgy galleries.

The sensational artist Joan Miró (1893–1983) felt such an affinity for his maternal homeland that he moved to Palma from his birth city, Barcelona. Mallorca's horizons and colours, the 'eloquent silence' and the patterns of Moorish and island folk art inspired his expressive, abstract work. Visit Miró's studio, just outside Palma in Cala Major, for an inspiring walk through his life and creativity. Then follow in his footsteps by taking the thrilling vintage train ride to **Sóller**, his mother's birthplace, where the train station has a brilliant room of his work (for free).

Right: *Ferrocarril de Sóller train cars in front of the Església de Sant Bartomeu, Sóller;* ***Opposite:*** *The Josep Lluís Sert–designed studio at Fundació Pilar i Joan Miró;* ***Next spread:*** *Inside the Miró studio.*

FUNDACIÓ PILAR I JOAN MIRÓ, CALA MAJOR

The highlight of Joan Miró's wonderful hilltop compound is the studio designed by his good friend, architect Josep Lluís Sert. This modern dream atelier looks as if Miró walked out yesterday: paintings, paint pots and mementos intact. The accompanying grand gallery and sculpture garden display some of the foundation's 2500 pieces of Miró's work.

FERROCARRIL DE SÓLLER

Step back in time on a vintage Ferrocarril de Sóller train from Palma, chugging through the Serra de Tramuntana to the Modernista city by the sea, Sóller. Linger in Sóller's train station, located in a historic mansion, for its free exhibition of gorgeous Miró prints. There's also a Picasso ceramics room.

VENICE, ITALY

Where art makes waves

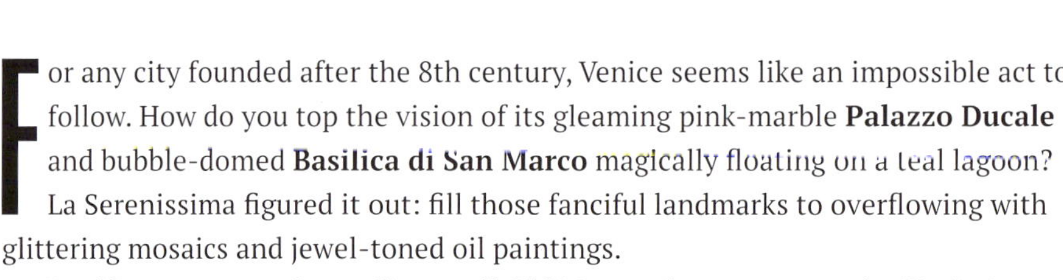

For any city founded after the 8th century, Venice seems like an impossible act to follow. How do you top the vision of its gleaming pink-marble **Palazzo Ducale** and bubble-domed **Basilica di San Marco** magically floating on a teal lagoon? La Serenissima figured it out: fill those fanciful landmarks to overflowing with glittering mosaics and jewel-toned oil paintings.

But if you're expecting wall-to-wall Old Masters here, guess again. Venice's grand old Gothic palaces have remained full of surprises ever since Peggy Guggenheim turned her Grand Canal palazzo into a launchpad for abstract expressionists and Italy's postwar revival. Inspired by the **Peggy Guggenheim Collection**, fashion moguls François Pinault and Miuccia Prada have cleverly installed their contemporary art finds along the Grand Canal at **Palazzo Grassi**, **Punta della Dogana** and **Fondazione Prada**.

Even alongside the Renaissance paintings gracing Palladio's **San Giorgio Maggiore**, you may find provocative artworks by Ai Weiwei installed by **Fondazione Giorgio Cini** curators – and it makes sense. Venetian Renaissance paintings often broke rules and defied censors, so avant-garde art seems right at home here. So if you miss a Biennale, never fear: this UNESCO World Heritage Site never runs out of fresh art.

WHEN TO GO

If possible, coincide with the Venice Art Biennale (spring to autumn in even-numbered years) or Venice Film Festival (first week of September).

GETTING THERE

Marco Polo (VCE) is Venice's mainland airport, and the main point of arrival for international (mostly Europe-based) airlines.

Below: *Lauren Halsey's keepers of the krown installation at the Venice Biennale;* **Left:** *Opulent Ca' Rezzonico, set in a Baldassare Longhena–designed palazzo on the Grand Canal.*

VENICE ART BIENNALE

Just when you think Venice can't possibly hold more art, in even-numbered years the city's Biennale throws open Giardini gates. Guest curators invite artists representing 100-plus countries to fill historic garden pavilions with site-specific contemporary art installations. And the world's most prestigious contemporary art expo keeps growing, taking over the boatyards at Venice's historic Arsenale.

CA' REZZONICO

For centuries this baroque Grand Canal palace set the Venetian standard for decadence, with heavenly ceilings and fanciful boudoir frescoes by Giambattista Tiepolo and his son Giandomenio. Today you're the lucky guest — check out ballroom concerts, an attic full of *vedutisti* (landscape artists), and sumptuous salons lined with winking portraits of socialites and their disapproving dogs by Rosalba Carriera and Pietro Longhi.

The art of survival

There's a secret to the extraordinary, dramatic output of Venetian Renaissance painters Bellini, Titian and Tintoretto: they lived longer. Reeling from the bubonic plague in the 15th century, the Venetian Republic consulted Mediterranean's top doctors and scientists, who determined that incoming ships should be kept at bay for *quaranta* (40) days. The world's first public-health quarantine worked – and Bellini, Titian and Tintoretto outlived and outpainted most Florentine Renaissance painters by decades. The artists showed monumental gratitude for their survival, covering the **Palazzo Ducale** with art extolling Venice's virtues and dedicating massive masterpieces to Venice's patron saints of plague protection at **Santa Maria della Salute** and **Scuola Grande di San Rocco**.

But the paintings that miraculously survived plague were almost lost to war. When he invaded Venice in 1797, greedy Napoleon tried to grab all its masterpieces that weren't bolted down – plus some that were, such as Veronese's *Marriage Feast at Cana* in **San Giorggio Maggiore**. Napoleon stockpiled sensuous Titians, stormy Tintorettos, angelic Bellinis and scandalous Veroneses at the Accademia – but his plans to take them home were foiled, and the **Gallerie dell'Accademia** is now open to non-emperors to enjoy. You can also swagger like Napoleon through dragon-frescoed halls of his imperial apartment at **Museo Correr**, and see the splendid **Marciana National Library** – decorated by Veronese, Titian and Tintoretto.

ROME, ITALY

Ancient city covered in art

WHEN TO GO

April to June and September to October are best – weather's good, festivals and outdoor events abound.

GETTING THERE

Fly to either Leonardo da Vinci-Fiumicino (FCO) or Ciampino (CIA) airports. Trains run to Rome's main Stazione Termini from across Italy and Europe.

Few cities rival Rome's astonishing artistic legacy. For millennia, it has starred in the great movements of European art, attracting the world's best artists and pushing the boundaries of creative achievement. The evidence is clear: the city overflows with priceless works of art, while ancient statues fill spectacular museums, and Byzantine mosaics and Renaissance frescoes cover art-rich churches.

The result of 3000 years of development, the cityscape is also an exhilarating sight. As you careen around town, you'll pass iconic structures such as the **Roman Forum**, **Colosseum** and **Pantheon**, demonstrating Rome's former status as *caput mundi* (capital of the world). Landmark basilicas demonstrate its importance as seat of the Catholic Church. Just look to St Peter's Basilica, soaring over it all, a material reminder of Rome's Renaissance popes and the genius of their ever-inventive architects.

Stroll through the centre and you'll encounter masterpieces along the way – Caravaggio paintings, Michelangelo sculptures and Raphael frescoes. Palazzos, such as grand Renaissance **Palazzo Farnese**, line medieval squares. Ornate piazzas flow with showy fountains: the **Fontana di Trevi** covering the entire side of 17th-century Palazzo Poli; or Bernini's **Fontana dei Quattro Fiumi** in Piazza Navona, adding a baroque flavour to the city's mesmerising streets.

VATICAN MUSEUMS

Walk 7km (4.3 miles) of galleries displaying Egyptian mummies, classical Greek and Roman sculptures and Etruscan bronzes, then follow up with abundant painted masterpieces, Raphael's resplendent frescoed rooms and Michelangelo's showstopping Sistine Chapel. Not to mention, the gardens.

CHIESA DI SAN LUIGI DEI FRANCESI

Pop into this elaborate baroque church to find a game-changing trio of Caravaggio paintings. Known collectively as the St Matthew Cycle, and painted between 1600 and 1602, they employ gripping chiaroscuro (the bold contrast of light and dark). Domenichino's faded 17th-century frescoes of St Cecilia and Guido Reni's altarpiece round out your visit.

Left: *Looking down on St Peter's Square and the Vatican Museums;* ***Above:*** *A riot of baroque within the Chiesa di San Luigi dei Francesi;* ***Opposite:*** *The (modern) Bramante Staircase within the Vatican Museums' Museo Pio-Clementino.*

Religious art in Rome

Popes, patrons and religious orders indelibly stamp Rome's art landscape. A tour through the city's myriad basilicas reveals a parade of sumptuous commissions. Rome's most important Jesuit church, **Chiesa del Gesù**, is a treasure of baroque art, including a swirling vault fresco by Giovanni Battista Gaulli, and Andrea del Pozzo's opulent tomb for Ignatius Loyola.

Basilica di Santa Maria del Popolo is one of Rome's richest Renaissance churches, and its outstanding art includes two Caravaggios, frescoes by Pinturicchio, and Caracci's *Assumption of the Virgin* (c 1660). Raphael designed the Cappella Chigi in 1514 and Bernini finished it 100 years later.

Crowning the summit of Esquiline Hill, the exterior of 5th-century **Basilica di Santa Maria Maggiore** glistens with 13th-century mosaics. Domenico Fontana built its own Cappella Sistina here in the 16th century, and it contains the tombs of popes Sixtus V and Pius V. Michelangelo created its Cappella Sforza.

Follow the many levels of Rome's art history at multilevelled **Basilica di San Clemente**. Descend from beautiful 15th-century Masolino frescoes and the 12th-century apse mosaic down to a 1st-century Roman house and dark 2nd-century temple to Mithras, with an altar showing the god slaying a bull. Beneath it all...the eerie burble of a subterranean river flowing through a Roman Republic–era channel.

ATHENS, GREECE

Ancient city, contemporary hotspot

WHEN TO GO
October through early April sees cooler weather, slightly fewer crowds. Mark your calendar for the Athens Biennale of Contemporary Art (usually in autumn).

GETTING THERE
Eleftherios Venizelos International Airport (ATH) is 27km (17 miles) east of Athens. Sail into ports of Piraeus or Rafina.

Cradle of Western civilisation and democracy, Athens is a hotbed of reinvention, serving up an anarchic mashup of architectural gravitas, urban grit and infectious creativity. The city's cultural and social life plays out amid, around and within landmarks that are centuries, if not millennia, old. The magnificent Acropolis – the citadel atop a rocky outcrop, crowned with temples fashioned from marble in the 5th century BCE – is the hub around which Athens still revolves.

But Athens is so much more than ancient ruins. Byzantine churches, Ottoman mosques and 19th-century neoclassical buildings contribute elegant architectural notes across the centre. Contemporary Athens pulses with vibrant energy and cultural relevancy – and nowhere is this more apparent than in its art offerings.

Support for cultural endeavours is often from philanthropic institutions such as the **Onassis Stegi** arts centre, run by the Onassis Foundation; and **NEON**, founded by art collector and entrepreneur Dimitris Daskalopoulos. Creative surprises lie around nearly every corner – quite literally, as Athens has also become one of Europe's top spots for **street art**.

Look out for pieces by local artists such as INO and Alexandros Vasmoulakis.

NATIONAL GALLERY

This incredible collection of Greek art from the 14th century to the present is hung in a state-of-the art building, which debuted in 2021. The spacious, light-filled galleries are arranged chronologically and thematically, with some of the real masterpieces being in the 20th-century collection. There are also 16th-century works here by Domenikos Theotokopoulos – aka El Greco.

NATIONAL ARCHAEOLOGICAL MUSEUM

The world's finest collection of Greek antiquities is housed in an enormous 19th-century neoclassical building. Its treasures, dating from prehistoric times to classical periods, offer a comprehensive view of Greek art and history. Exquisite sculptures, pottery, jewellery, frescoes and artefacts, found throughout Greece and beyond, are displayed mainly thematically.

Above: *The Jockey of Artemision, galloping through the galleries of the National Archaeological Museum;* ***Opposite:*** *Looking across Athens from the Odeon of Herodes Atticus toward the Acropolis.*

The Benaki Museum

The Benaki Museum, spread across seven locations – six of which are in Athens – has an outstanding collection of over 120,000 artworks from the Paleolithic to the modern day. It was founded by art collector Antonis Benakis, scion of one of the prominent families of the Greek diaspora, who was born in Alexandria in 1873. The flagship branch is the **Benaki Museum of Greek Culture**, occupying one of Athens' most beautiful neoclassical-style buildings. Come here to view Byzantine icons and an extensive collection of Greek regional costumes, as well as complete sitting rooms from Macedonian mansions, intricately carved and painted. Benakis had such a good eye that even the agricultural tools are beautiful. The terrace cafe has a splendid view of the National Garden and the Acropolis.

The Benaki's **Ghika Gallery** includes the preserved apartment and atelier of Nikos Hadjikyriakos-Ghika (1906–94) – a fascinating insight into the life and inspirations of one of Greece's great modern artists. Many of Ghika's works are on display, including vivid sketches he made on his international travels. There are also three floors of galleries devoted to other influential 20th-century Greek artists, photographers, poets, actors and architects – a real who's who of the nation's creative talent.

MUSEUMS & GALLERIES

Acropolis Museum
Eyeball the original Parthenon Marbles and five Caryatids from the Acropolis

Allouche Benias Gallery
Contemporary art shows in a beautifully restored neoclassical mansion

Basil & Elise Goulandris Foundation
Works by pioneering Greek painters, as well as the likes of Picasso and Bacon

Benaki Museum: Pireos 138
Temporary exhibitions focusing on the contemporary and inventive

Byzantine & Christian Museum
Replete with religious art, including icons and delicate frescoes

Dio Horia Gallery
Post-digital art, queer art, female empowerment, new technological media

EMST: National Museum of Contemporary Art
Former FIX brewery transformed into contemporary art gallery

Kanellopoulos Museum
Neoclassical mansion containing lovely classical and Byzantine art and jewellery

Loverdos Museum
Beautifully restored townhouse showcasing post-Byzantine religious art

Museum Alex Mylona
Super-minimalist sculpture and paintings by Athenian grande dame Alex Mylona

Museum of Cycladic Art
Dedicated to the iconic marble Cycladic figurines, some dating back to 3000 BCE

Benaki Museum: Museum of Islamic Art
Branch of the Benaki, houses a significant collection of Islamic art

National Historical Museum
Eclectic collection housed in the handsome Old Parliament Building.

Numismatic Museum
Gorgeous Ernst Ziller–designed mansion, housing an impressive coin collection

Vorres Museum
Contemporary, folk and traditional art in a beautiful out-of-town setting

Left: *The National Library at the Stavros Niarchos Foundation Cultural Center;* ***Above:*** *The iconic Caryatids support the south portal of the Acropolis' Erechtheion;* ***Opposite:*** *Pieces from Maja Djordjevic's Theatre of Memories show at the Dio Horia Gallery.*

ARCHITECTURE

Acropolis Museum
Amazing building designed by Bernard Tschumi, alongside Greek architect Michael Photiadis

Anafiotika
Architecturally distinct enclave of whitewashed island-style houses in Plaka

Ancient Agora
Frequented both by Socrates and St Paul; home to the grand Temple of Hephaistos

Church of Agios Eleftherios
The exterior is a mix of medieval beasts and ancient gods in bas-relief

Church of Agios Dimitrios Loumbardiaris
Lovely 16th-century church at foot of Filopappou Hill

Mosque of Tzistarakis
Built in 1759, this is one of Athens' few surviving mosques

National Gallery
Award-winning building that affords glorious skyline views from its floor-to-ceiling windows

Neoclassical 'Trilogy'
Handsome side-by-side trio of Athens Academy, Athens University and the National Library

Odeon of Herodes Atticus
Large amphitheatre, built in 161 CE and still used for performances

Onassis Stegi
Contemporary arts centre that glows like a giant lantern at night

Panathenaic Stadium
Ancient-turned-modern 70,000-seater stadium built into Ardettos Hill

Parliament
Built as the royal palace of Otto, first king of modern Greece

Parthenon
Pre-eminent Acropolis monument and largest ever Doric temple in Greece

Stavros Niarchos Foundation Cultural Center
Renzo Piano–designed home to the Greek National Opera and National Library

Technopolis
Impressively restored 1862 gasworks, now a cultural venue

Tower of the Winds
Beautiful pentelic-marble tower within the Roman Agora

CYPRUS

Art spanning the divide

NICOSIA (LEFKOSIA),

WHEN TO GO

April–May and September–October, for the pleasant temperatures and smaller crowds.

GETTING THERE

The Greek Republic of Cyprus has international airports at Larnaka (LCA) and Pafos (PFO); North Cyprus' Ercan (ECN) can only be reached via Türkiye.

Europe's last divided capital, Nicosia (Lefkosia) comes at art from two different perspectives, one Greek and one Turkish, but younger Cypriot artists are using their creativity to bring communities together. Funding from the UN and other international bodies has given extra vim to art projects on both sides of the Green Line dividing Nicosia into Greek and Turkish enclaves.

In the heart of old Nicosia, surprising art spaces spill out of tangled medieval lanes, providing a contemporary counterpoint to the ancient ceramics, sculptures and religious paintings inside the **Cyprus Museum**, **Leventis Museum** and **Byzantine Museum**.

In the south, the **Nicosia Municipal Arts Centre (NiMAC)** is the hub for an arty district buzzing with exhibitions, talks and screenings. North of the Green Line, **Side Streets** explores ideas about language, art and culture, while the **ARUCAD Art Space** shows the output of the Arkin University of Creative Arts and Design.

Small galleries selling work by local artists pop up all over Nicosia – stencil artist Christos Kakoulli's **Gallery 37** and **Diachroniki** are rewarding stops. Don't overlook the outspoken street art blossoming around the Green Line, and the sprawling new city beyond the Venetian walls, home to innovative art spaces such as **Stand in Line**.

NICOSIA MUNICIPAL ARTS CENTRE (NiMAC)

Housed in a former power plant in the mazelike lanes of Old Nicosia, NiMAC hosts shows of paintings, photography, sculpture, installations and video art, asking some probing questions about Cyprus' cultural and political trajectory. A hip restaurant and expansive art library provide extra reasons to linger.

BYZANTINE MUSEUM

The medieval religious paintings, mosaics and frescoes displayed at this atmospheric space inside the Archbishop's Palace compound include treasures looted from Northern Cyprus and later seized back from the international art black market. It's a vital link between contemporary Cypriot art and the ancient works displayed inside the Cyprus Museum.

Above: *Divided by the Green Line, Nicosia (Lefkosia) is home to both Greek-style churches and minaret-topped mosques;* ***Opposite:*** *Ancient religious artworks displayed in the Byzantine Museum.*

Art from the ancestors

Don't look at the **Cyprus Museum** merely as a collection of excavated artefacts; think of it as a map of the island's artistic journey. On display are treasures from one of Europe's most creative cultures, dating from the Byzantine period all the way back to prehistory. Everything on show was found within Cyprus' borders – a testament to the artistic richness of this sun-blessed Mediterranean island.

Some of Europe's most iconic prehistoric art was created by ancient Cypriots, including the surprisingly modern-looking sculptural forms of the Lemba fertility figurines, created 5000 years before Henry Moore explored similar ground in the arty enclave of London's Hampstead Village.

The sculptural magnificence of ancient Greece and Rome is impressively represented in marble, bronze and stone, but it's the 2500-year-old ceramics that grip the imagination, adorned with everything from paintings of Greek legends to stylised depictions of birds, octopuses and abstract patterns of dots and rings that could have sprung from a 1920s modernist pottery workshop.

After touring the galleries, head over to the **Leventis Municipal Museum of Nicosia** inside the city walls, home to the island's most impressive collection of cartoonlike, medieval sgraffito pottery, created while the island was governed by Crusader knights.

YEREVAN, ARMENIA

One big gallery of Armenian art

WHEN TO GO

Spring and autumn are the most pleasant, but any time is good for art lovers.

GETTING THERE

Yerevan's Zvartnots International Airport (EVN) hosts flights from Europe and the Middle East. Land borders are only open between Georgia and Iran.

Once a great empire, the Armenian nation spread across the world in a diaspora that stretched as far as India, Jerusalem and California. After the fall of the Soviet Union, Armenia became a modern country and numerous diasporites returned – many of them bringing back invaluable art to its capital, Yerevan.

Start your art tour of this culture-lovers' paradise by circling the grand, tufa-stone Republic Sq and its captivating musical fountains before entering the **National Art Gallery**. Here you'll find celebrated Armenian painters over multiple floors, plus precious carpets that date back centuries and the world's oldest leather shoe. Carry on to the Romanesque **Opera Theatre and Ballet**, which hosts superb, great-value performances. Then check out Yerevan's many galleries – such as **Martiros Sarian House**, **Ervand Kochar Museum** and **Sergei Parajanov Museum** – which pay tribute to groundbreaking Armenian artists. Yerevan's burgeoning contemporary art scene is incredible, too; experience it at the **Modern Art Museum** and **Mirzoyan Library** – a photo-book library, hip cafe and bar.

Before you leave, touch base with the musical side of the city at **Charles Aznavour Sq**, a landmark that honours the French-Armenian vibrato tenor of *La Bohème* fame, and catch a jazz show at Ulikhanyan Club.

CAFESJIAN CENTRE FOR THE ARTS

At 302m (991ft) high and covering an area of 13 hectares (32 acres), the Cafesjian Centre for the Arts is more than a brutalist monument to the Soviet Union. Known as the 'Cascade' for its tumbling staircase, the pyramid-like structure has been reimagined as a spectacular contemporary art gallery, sculpture garden and the perfect place to watch a sunset.

MATENADARAN

Immensely important to Armenians, the Matenadaran book depository houses 23,000 manuscripts, documents and maps that date back to the 7th century. While only some of the books are on display, all are a wonder to look at, many with delicate illustrations and fine ivory and precious-metal covers.

Right: *The Matenadaran, repository of Armenia's most precious books and manuscripts;* ***Above:*** *Fernando Botero's Woman Smoking a Cigarette in the Cafesjian Centre for the Arts complex;* ***Opposite:*** *Yerevan's cityscape from the Cafesjian gardens.*

Sergei Parajanov

Sergei Parajanov's 1969 film *The Colour of Pomegranates* is a trip. The Armenian artist's mostly silent cinematic interpretation of the life of 18th-century bard Sayat-Nova is heaped in symbolism – like the lead character milking a llama in a monastery. Some say Parajanov's intent was to highlight the resilience of Armenian culture. Whatever he was thinking, many rank the film as one of the most influential movies of all time and Parajanov in the echelon of revolutionary directors.

Born in Tbilisi to Armenian parents, Parajanov dabbled in music, film, collage and controversy – his choice to make his 1965 movie *Shadows of Forgotten Ancestors* in a Ukrainian dialect rather than dubbed in Russian put him in Moscow's crosshairs. He was sent to a Soviet prison from 1974–78 and again in 1982 on trumped-up charges of homosexuality, bribery and 'incitement to suicide'. Protest from international artists led to Parajanov's release, and he died in Yerevan in 1990 at the age of 66.

Visit Yerevan's **Sergei Parajanov Museum** for a mind-bending journey through the eccentric artist's strange and stimulating work. There are riffs on the *Mona Lisa*, collages of dinnerware shards and tiny 'thalers', as Parajanov called them: faces that he carved into aluminium milk-bottle lids with his fingertips while in prison.

Փարաջանով

Above: *Katherine Bertram's The Skin I Am In at the World of WearableArt (WOW), New Zealand/Aotearoa;* ***Opposite:*** *Randy Polumbo's Grotto at Hobart's Museum of Old and New Art, Australia.*

OCEANIA

KAKADU NATIONAL PARK, AUSTRALIA

World-famous Aboriginal rock art

WHEN TO GO

Kakadu National Park is most easily accessed during the dry season (May–October).

GETTING THERE

The national park's two main rock-art sites are both a three-hour, 285km (177-mile) drive east of Darwin.

A vital part of Australia's First Nations cultures, rock art offers an intriguing window into how humans lived and thought on this continent as far back as 40,000 years ago, when the first works were created.

Researchers estimate that there are more than 100,000 significant rock-art sites around Australia. But the richly decorated rock shelves of **Kakadu National Park**, created with pigments from iron-rich ochre clays, steal the spotlight. Not only are there plenty of well-preserved works to be seen in this remote Top End wilderness, but the 'X-ray' art style traditionally used by the Indigenous artists of this region depicts subjects including both now-extinct wildlife and Creation (Dreaming) beings in incredible anatomical detail, offering unique insights into the artists' connections to their Country (traditional lands) since time immemorial.

Interpretative signage at Kakadu's two largest and most accessible rock-art sites help to contextualise the significance of the vibrant works before you, but these paintings are layered with enough stories to fill a thousand signboards. Join a Bininj (local Aboriginal) ranger-guided tour of Ubirr or Burrungkuy (Nourlangie) during the dry season to connect more deeply with the artistic legacy of your guide's ancestors.

***Right:** Ubirr is home to a wealth of rock-art images painted in X-ray, which became the dominant style here some 8000 years ago; **Opposite:** 'Contact art' at the Nanguluwurr Gallery, Burrungkuy (Nourlangie).*

UBIRR

The layers of rock art spread over Ubirr's five main galleries are a visual feast. Part of the main gallery reads like a menu, with images of kangaroos, tortoises and fish painted in X-ray, which became the dominant style about 8000 years ago. Predating these are intriguing paintings of Mimi Spirits (Creation Ancestors).

BURRUNGKUY (NOURLANGIE)

A 1.5km (0.9-mile) loop walk takes in several rock-art sites including the Anbangbang Gallery, featuring vivid Dreaming characters such as Namarrkon (Lightning Man). On the northern side of Burrungkuy, a longer trail leads to the Nanguluwurr Gallery, where the rock art includes a good example of 'contact art' – a painting of a two-masted sailing ship.

MELBOURNE, AUSTRALIA

Bursts of colour around every corner

WHEN TO GO

Summer (December–February) is a great time. Avoid October, the wettest month.

GETTING THERE

Some of the best art experiences are right in the centre of the city, which is is a 30-minute drive from Melbourne Airport (MEL). Take a taxi, rideshare or the Skybus.

Everyone seems to be an artist in Melbourne/Naarm. Australia's second-largest city is a magnet for creatives drawn to its vibrant fashion, music and contemporary art scenes. Visitors will find many of Melbourne's cultural institutions within easy strolling distance, in the very heart of the city.

Wander from the street-art-splattered lanes of the inner city into Federation Sq. It's home to such cultural institutions as **Koorie Heritage Trust**, with First Nations art and events; the **Australian Centre for the Moving Image (ACMI)**, celebrating screen culture; and the **Ian Potter Centre**, housing the **National Gallery of Victoria**'s Australian collection. Federation Sq itself is an architectural landmark and gathering space that can house 15,000 people. Built entirely over dense railway lines beside the river, it's constructed using tessellating pinwheels in sandstone, zinc and coloured glass, resulting in something that looks a bit like a sci-fi cathedral. Cross the river to explore the stunning collection at the **Australian Centre for Contemporary Art (ACCA)**, or jump on a tram or train to discover other creative precincts: **Footscray Community Arts Centre** is a hub for cultural diversity and community arts, or venture to the live-music hotbeds of Fitzroy and St Kilda.

LANEWAY ART

The city centre is a labyrinth of laneways adorned with colourful artworks. Look out for murals, stencils, paste-ups, stickers and hidden sculptures. The most famous lanes include AC/DC Lane, named after the seminal Aussie rock band and home to music-inspired work, including a wall sculpture of singer Bon Scott. There's also atmospheric Centre Place, packed with cafes and edgy art; and cobbled, street-art-famous Hosier Lane.

NGV INTERNATIONAL

For a peek at the establishment, head down St Kilda Rd to the impressive brutalist building housing the NGV International, Australia's oldest and most-visited gallery. The 70,000-work collection includes pieces by Rembrandt, Dalí and William Blake. Plus, it's all free!

***Left:** Street-art-swathed Hosier Lane; **Above:** Steen Jones' Melbourne rose mural, on AC/DC Lane in the CBD; **Opposite:** Brighton Bathing Boxes on Dendy Street Beach, backdropped by the city skyline.*

Heide: cradle of Australian modernism

Today, Bulleen is deep in Melbourne suburbia. But back in 1934, when John and Sunday Reed purchased an old dairy farm on a lovely bend of the Birrarung/Yarra River, it was an idyllic rural retreat.

The Reeds were patrons of the arts and the old dairy, which they named Heide, soon became the epicentre of Australian modernism. They opened their home to landmark artists, including Arthur Boyd, Albert Tucker, Charles Blackman, Sidney Nolan and Joy Hester.

The Heide Circle was also a hotbed of radical politics and sexual experimentation, with the avant-garde Reeds, who had an open relationship, at its centre. They sponsored Sidney Nolan's series of Ned Kelly paintings, and co-published the *Angry Penguins* cultural journal with surrealist poet Max Harris.

Angry Penguins was the victim of Australia's most famous literary hoax: the Ern Malley affair. The journal published a series of 'fake' surrealist poems by the made-up poet Ern Malley. Though it was a humiliation for *Angry Penguins* (and Max Harris was tried for obscenity), some critics have applauded the hoax as a surrealist masterpiece in its own right.

Today the old farmhouse and the stunning new modernist home the Reeds built (Heide II) are open as the Heide Museum of Modern Art.

TASMANIA, AUSTRALIA

An island of inimitable art

WHEN TO GO
Summer (December–February) is popular for visiting this oft-chilly state, but winter (June–August) brings food and wine festivals.

GETTING THERE
The *Spirit of Tasmania* ferries mainlanders to Devonport overnight, while flights reach Hobart (HBA) and Launceston (LST) from across Australia.

The transformation of Tasmania (lutruwita) into an artistic powerhouse is often credited to **MONA**, the **Museum of Old and New Art**. But Australia's island state has long been fertile ground for creativity.

Hidden away in the Tasmanian Wilderness World Heritage Area – a realm of temperate rainforests, thrashing rivers and wind-battered coast – are the island's original artworks, created by Aboriginal people more than 15,000 years ago. These hand-stencilled patterns are immortalised in ochre and blood on the walls of caves such as **Ballawinne** and remote **Wargata Mina**. Traditional styles and techniques still influence Tasmania's present-day Aboriginal artists, whose work can be admired (and bought) in commercial galleries like **Art Mob** in the state capital, Hobart.

Elsewhere, local artists have channelled their relative isolation into landscape painting, like David Keeling's studies of lonely shores and spidery eucalyptus branches; find his work at Hobart's **TMAG**, and the **Queen Victoria Museum and Art Gallery (QVMAG)** in Tassie's second city, Launceston. Meanwhile the Tasmanian Gothic – the island's own dark romanticism, wrapped up in its distinctive landscape – whispers

through Pat Brassington's dreamlike photographs (also on show at TMAG). Small towns twinkle with creativity, too: mural-splashed Sheffield is practically an open-air gallery.

MONA (MUSEUM OF OLD & NEW ART)

Hobart-born polymath David Walsh designed a gambling system that won millions, then spent it on eyebrow-raising art. The result is MONA, a warren of wall-mounted vulvas, voluptuous race cars and risqué religious art. MONA also courted controversy with its now closed Ladies Lounge gallery and turned the resulting court proceedings into performance art. Undeniably original.

TMAG (TASMANIAN MUSEUM & ART GALLERY)

Hobart's TMAG gallery complex showcases a skinned Tasmanian tiger (the state's now-extinct emblem) alongside 19th-century decorative arts and rotating exhibitions. Following a public apology for past treatment of Aboriginal artefacts, TMAG now confronts its colonial past and hosts the First Peoples Art and Culture collection: 12,000 artworks from across the Asia-Pacific region and beyond.

Above: *MONA's tranquil waterside setting on the Derwent River north of Hobart;* ***Opposite:*** *TMAG's mapiya lumi ('around here') childrens' gallery, telling Tasmania's story with tactile exhibits.*

WELLINGTON, NEW ZEALAND/ AOTEAROA

A very cool little capital

WHEN TO GO
Wellington is generally warm and pleasant November–March; it can get cold and wet May–August.

GETTING THERE
Fly into Wellington International Airport (WLG) domestically or direct from major Australian cities. Wellington is the North Island's port for inter-island ferries.

Compact when compared with other international capitals, central Wellington celebrates the energy of a much bigger city. Almost smack dab in the middle of the country – thanks to a historic compromise for the site of the capital – there's a lot going on in terms of the arts.

Even New Zealand's parliament building, nicknamed the 'Beehive', resembles a massive art installation. (The city nickname 'Windy Welly' suggests strong gales, but Kiwis know that 'Windy Welly' also refers to the bluster from politicians living in the capital.)

The city's other nickname is 'Wellywood', thanks to the successes of film director Peter Jackson, special-effects company Wētā Workshop and the *Lord of the Rings* trilogy. Drop into the moviemaking museum **Wētā Cave** for a tour.

The harbour waterfront is dominated by **Te Papa Tongarewa**, the National Museum, plus a host of innovative and playful art pieces. Hip Cuba St is renowned for its cafes (don't miss revolutionary Fidel's), bars and a kinetic sculpture, the *Bucket Fountain* – from which a bucket is occasionally purloined on a raucous Saturday night. Wellington also claims to be Aotearoa's craft-beer capital, with hoppy adventures available to pioneering breweries such as Garage Project, Parrotdog and Tuatara.

WORLD OF WEARABLEART (WOW)
Wellington's gain was Nelson's loss when this phenomenally successful international design event outgrew the South Island regional city. These days WOW – which prides itself as being the 'most lavish catwalk in the world' – is held over three weeks from late September.

RITA ANGUS COTTAGE
Built in 1877, this tiny cottage in Thorndon was the home of Rita Angus, one of New Zealand's best-known painters, from 1955 until her death in 1970. The house, garden, Thorndon and Wellington all feature in her work, and the cottage is now used as a residency for visiting artists. It can be viewed from the street at 194a Sydney St West, Thorndon.

Above: *Grace DuVal's Curves Ahead at the World of Wearableart (WOW);* ***Opposite:*** *Fidel's Cafe on Wellington's Cuba St.*

Te Papa Tongarewa & the Wharf Precinct

At the southern end of Wellington's waterfront, Te Papa Tongarewa is New Zealand's impressive national museum – known simply as Te Papa. The name loosely translates as 'treasure box' and the riches inside include an amazing collection of Māori artefacts, a colourful *marae* (meeting house) and a selection of excellent exhibitions and galleries: Toi Art showcases the national art collection and contemporary work from local artists.

Wellington's Wharf Precinct, to the north of Te Papa, features some equally impressive art treasures. **City Gallery** hosts one-off exhibitions and supports emerging Kiwi artists in Wellington's former public library, built in 1940 in an Art Deco style. Harbourside, **Māori Arts Gallery** sells traditional Māori jewellery and carvings made from bone and *pounamu* (greenstone). **Wellington Museum**, in an 1892 waterfront bond store, presents an imaginative and interactive experience of the city's social and maritime history, while the **New Zealand Academy of Fine Arts** exhibits NZ artists, from canvasses and drawings to ceramics and photography. The **New Zealand Portrait Gallery** is housed in a heritage red-brick warehouse. For walking tours and harbour paddles from a Māori perspective, visit Te Wharewaka o Pōneke; their trips out into the harbour in traditionally carved working *waka* (canoes) are an absolute highlight.

NOUMÉA, NEW CALEDONIA

French style in the South Pacific

WHEN TO GO

Best May–October, during the South Pacific's cooler months; November–April is hot, humid and cyclone-season.

GETTING THERE

Fly to New Caledonia's gateway, La Tontouta International Airport (NOU), 37km (23 miles) northwest of Nouméa.

While most turn up to enjoy this South Pacific paradise's dazzling World Heritage–listed lagoon, New Caledonia isn't just a tropical playground. It's a charming mix of French and Melanesian culture: warm hospitality and elegance, gourmet food beneath palm trees, glorious sand, warm waters, resorts and bungalows.

Nouméa, the cosmopolitan capital, on the main island of Grande-Terre, is both sophisticated and uncomplicated, classy and casual. Diners can eat out at sassy French restaurants hidden in Quartier Latin and at bold waterfront bistros, or grab a bargain meal from a food truck in a car park. Shopaholics can splurge on the latest Parisian fashions or go bargain hunting for imported Asian textiles or local crafts. The urban landscape is adorned with diverse outdoor artworks, from towering Kanak sculptures to mural frescoes.

The central city revolves around Place des Cocotiers, a large, shady square of landscaped gardens with a band rotunda, massive chessboard and pétanque pitches. The **Musée de la Ville de Nouméa** is right on the square, with the **Tjibaou Cultural Centre** to the north of the city centre. South of the centre, Baie des Citrons and Anse Vata feature lovely beaches, restaurants, bars and nightclubs. Offshore islands well worth visiting include otherworldly Île des Pins and, further afield, the three Loyalty Islands of Lifou, Maré and Ouvéa.

***Right:** The French tricolour flies above the Musée de la Ville de Nouméa; **Opposite:** Renzo Piano's soaring Tjibaou Cultural Centre was inspired by traditional Kanak architecture; **Next spread:** Kanak and Oceanian contemporary art on display at the Tjibaou.*

TJIBAOU CULTURAL CENTRE

A tribute to pro-independence Kanak leader Jean-Marie Tjibaou, who was assassinated in 1989, this masterpiece of tall, curved wooden structures rises majestically above the trees. Designed by Italian architect Renzo Piano, its harmony between the contemporary architecture and the surrounding landscape is mesmerising. Inside, Kanak culture is represented by sculptures, paintings and photographs.

MUSEE DE LA VILLE DE NOUMÉA

The French-style Musée de la Ville de Nouméa, in a beautiful, historic 1874 building that was New Caledonia's first bank, features fascinating displays and artwork on the early history of Nouméa and is lit up each December for the Lights Festival (Fête de la Lumière).

TOP 10 LISTS

TOP FANTASTIC PLACES TO VISIT ARTISTS' HOMES

1 Maputo, Mozambique (Malangatana Valente Ngwenya)

2 New York State, USA (Hudson Valley: Frederic Church and Thomas Cole; Manhattan: Donald Judd)

3 Santa Fe, New Mexico, USA (Georgia O'Keeffe)

4 San Francisco, California, USA (David Ireland)

5 Mexico City, Mexico (Frida Kahlo, Diego Rivera, Leonora Carrington, Luis Barragán)

6 Oslo, Norway (Edvard Munch)

7 United Kingdom (London: JMW Turner, Frederic Lord Leighton; Cornwall: Barbara Hepworth; Glasgow: Charles Rennie Mackintosh and Margaret Macdonald)

8 France (Paris: Eugène Delacroix; Giverny: Claude Monet; Antibes: Pablo Picasso; Aix-en-Provence: Cézanne)

9 Mallorca, Spain (Joan Miró)

10 Wellington, New Zealand/Aotearoa (Rita Angus)

Clockwise, from below: *Old Cairo souqs, Egypt; Museo Casa Estudio Diego Rivera y Frida Kahlo, Mexico City, Mexico; Judd Foundation, New York City, USA.*

TEN GREAT PLACES TO SEE FOLK ART

1. Old Cairo souqs, Egypt
2. American Folk Art Museum, New York City, USA
3. Museum of International Folk Art, Santa Fe, New Mexico, USA
4. Oaxaca, Mexico
5. Antigua, Guatemala
6. Japan Folk Crafts Museum, Tokyo, Japan
7. Seoul Museum of Craft Art, Seoul, South Korea
8. Reykjavík, Iceland
9. Wereldmuseum Amsterdam, Netherlands
10. Mallorca, Spain

TEN FAMILY-FRIENDLY MUSEUMS

1. Grand Egyptian Museum, Cairo, Egypt
2. Metropolitan Museum of Art, New York City, New York, USA
3. Meow Wolf, Santa Fe, New Mexico, USA
4. Exploratorium, San Francisco, California, USA
5. Ghibli Museum, Tokyo, Japan
6. National Gallery Singapore, Singapore
7. Wereldmuseum Amsterdam, Netherlands
8. Tate Modern, London, England
9. Musée du Louvre, Paris, France
10. Wētā Cave, Wellington, New Zealand/Aotearoa

Clockwise, from above: *Giza's Great Pyramid of Khufu, Egypt; Meow Wolf, Santa Fe, USA; The Exploratorium in San Francisco, USA.*

TEN PIECES OF ART FOR YOUR BUCKET LIST

1. Great Pyramid of Khufu, Giza, Egypt
2. Art House Project, Naoshima, Japan
3. *Cloud Gate* (aka 'The Bean') by Anish Kapoor, Chicago, Illinois, USA
4. *Prada Marfa* by Elmgreen & Dragset, Marfa, Texas, USA
5. Moai stone heads, Rapa Nui (Easter Island), Chile
6. *The Kiss* by Gustav Klimt, Upper Belvedere Palace, Vienna, Austria
7. Gaudí's La Sagrada Família, Barcelona, Spain
8. Michelangelo's Sistine Chapel, Vatican Museums, Rome, Italy
9. Aboriginal rock art, Kakadu National Park, Northern Territory, Australia
10. Sand drawing, Vanuatu

TEN PHENOMENAL PLACES FOR STREET ART

1 Maputo, Mozambique
2 İstanbul, Türkiye
3 Detroit, Michigan, USA
4 Valparaíso, Chile
5 Tokyo, Japan
6 Penang, Malaysia
7 Manila, Philippines
8 Cologne, Germany
9 Athens, Greece
10 Wimmera-Mallee, Australia

Clockwise, from below: *Venice Art Biennale, Italy; Penang, Malaysia; Valparaíso, Chile.*

TEN INCREDIBLE SITE-SPECIFIC ARTWORKS

1. *Shadows Travelling on the Sea of the Day* by Olafur Eliasson, Northern Qatar
2. Gorée Island, Senegal
3. *Yellow Pumpkin* by Yayoi Kusama, Naoshima, Japan
4. Docking Seoul, Seoul, South Korea
5. Venice Art Biennale, Italy
6. New York City Subway Permanent Art Collection, New York, USA
7. Heidelberg Project, Detroit, Michigan, USA
8. Bay Bridge Lights, San Francisco, California, USA
9. *Čumil* by Viktor Hulík, Bratislava, Slovakia
10. *Maman* by Louise Bourgeois, Tokyo, Japan

G

H

I

J

T

U

V

W

Y

Z

PHOTO CREDITS

Cover: Vicente Manuel Rosas Pereyna, "Vincitore", 2010, reed wood and paper (china paper), photo Sun_Shine/Shutterstock; **4-5:** 2024 Nucleo Storico, photo Marco Zorzanello. Courtesy Archivio Storico della Biennale di Venezia, ASAC; **8:** Andrés Reisinger GC AR Take Over Jeddah Physical Installation, photo Karina Perez Spritze, Rhose Studio; **9:** Installation views, 'Selections from the Collection', courtesy of Zeitz MOCAA, photo Dillon Marsh; **10:** View Pictures/Hufton+Crow/Universal Images Group via Getty Images; **11:** Installation views, 'Selections from the Collection', courtesy of Zeitz MOCAA, photo Dillon Marsh; **12:** © NPL - DeA Picture Library/S. Vannini/Bridgeman Images 13: Dale Johnson/500px; **14:** Imago/ Alamy; **15:** Xinhua News Agency via Getty Images; **16:** Emmanuelle Andrianjafy for Lonely Planet; **17:** Na Chainkua Reindorf, Strange Flesh, solo show at Galerie Cécile Fakhoury, Dakar, Senegal, May, 2024, Courtesy of the artist and Galerie Cécile Fakhoury, photo Morel Sedani; **18:** Galerie Arte, photo Joelle Le Bussy; **19:** Emmanuelle Andrianjafy for Lonely Planet; **20:** © Jardin Majorelle, photo Nicolas Mathéus; **21:** 1-54 Marrakech 2023. © Adnane Zemmama, Katherine E. Knecht/Shutterstock; **22-23:** Gardens by Design/Shutterstock; **24:** Close up of the work 'Spiritualité I', 'Fraternité', Diadji Diop solo exhibition (2023)/ © Comptoir des Mines Galerie; **25:** 'Qui tiendra l'Afrique tiendra le Ciel' (Whoever holds Africa will hold the Sky), Building details /Exhibition, Mohamed Arejdal (2019)/ © Comptoir des Mines Galerie; **26:** Leshiy985/Shutterstock; **27:** Sculpies/Getty Images, Lensfield/Shutterstock; **28:** Akimov Konstantin/Shutterstock; **29:** Emily M Wilson/Getty Images; **30:** ZZ3701/iStock; **31:** Creativity Lover/Shutterstock, Jon Arnold/AWL Images; **32:** Neil McAllister/Alamy; **33:** Eric Lafforgue/ Art in All of Us/Getty Images; **34:** Face of the city (2023), Mohammed Alfaraj, The Hayy Jameel Façade Commission/ Courtesy of Art Jameel; **35:** Julio Lafuente, The Four Lanterns, 1970s, photo Hany Musallam/Shutterstock; **36:** Balad Al Fann photo Emad Alhusayni; **37:** Nour Abdullah Gary, Daily Train of Thought, 2023, photography, Sindbad I Can See Land Exhibition, Balad Al Fann; **38:** The Museum of Islamic Art, Doha / Qatar Museums; **39:** رفس راهنلا رحب يف للاظلا (Shadows travelling on the sea of the day), 2022 | Installation view: Northern Heritage sites, Doha, 2022 | photo Iwan Baan | Courtesy of the artist | neugerriemschneider, Berlin | Tanya Bonakdar Gallery, New York / Los Angeles © 2022 Olafur Eliasson; **40-41:** The new National Museum of Qatar designed by Ateliers Jean Nouvel, photo Iwan Baan; **42:** Mehmet O/Shutterstock; **43:** Istanbul Modern, photo Cemal Emden, BULENT KILIC/AFP/ GettyImages; **44:** Xantana/Getty Images; **45:** Mark Read for Lonely Planet; **46:** Alexander Demyanenko/Shutterstock; **47:** People Amongst the People, 2008, Susan Point, photo Michael Wheatley/Alamy; **48:** Aksadjuak, Roger | Aksadjuak, Laurent. Canadian/Canadian (Rankin Inlet), 1972–2014, Spring Celebration, 1996, clay 54 x 48.3 x 47.2 cm. Collection of the Winnipeg Art Gallery acquired with funds from George William Battershill in memory of his wife Helen Battershill, 2002-90. Photo: Ernest Mayer, courtesy of WAG-Qaumajuq; **49:** WAG-Qaumajuq Building, photo Lindsay Reid, courtesy of WAG-Qaumajuq; **50:** Bill Reid's The Raven and the First Men, photo Goh Iromoto, courtesy of the Museum of Anthropology at UBC; **51:** Museum of Anthropology Great Hall, photo Cory Dawson, courtesy of the Museum of Anthropology at UBC, Apexphotos/Getty Images; **52:** Blanketing The City IV: Cathedral Square, Debra Sparrow, photo Michael Wheatley/Alamy, BC Place, Debra Sparrow, Blanketing the City, Winter Arts Festival, photo Mavreen David; **54:** Terryfic3D/Getty Images; **55:** Arlene Shechet, Bea Blue, 2024. Courtesy of the Artist and Pace Gallery. Installation view of Arlene Shechet: Girl Group at Storm King Art Center, photo David Schulze; **56:** Matt Munro for Lonely Planet; **57:** Brooklyn Chic mural by David Elmo Cooper, photo Leonard Zhukovsky/ Shutterstock; **58:** Felieke van der Leest. Rainbow Moose (sculpture with necklace) (edition of 3), 2005. © 2024 Artists Rights Society (ARS), New York / BONO, Oslo, photo Bruce M. White; **59:** Museum of Arts and Design, photo Gustav Liliequist. Courtesy Museum of Arts and Design; **61:** © Estate of Jean Dubuffet, ADAGP Paris / IVARO Dublin, 2025, photo Guillaume Gaudet/Lonely Planet, Solomon R. Guggenheim Museum, photo Michele Falzone/Getty Images, MoMA, photo Athanasios Gioumpasis/Getty Images, Tony Rosenthal, Alamo, 1967, courtesy of the Estate of Tony Rosenthal, photo Holly Vegter/Shutterstock; **62:** Installation view, Keith Haring. Courtesy of Rubell Museum, Miami, photo Chi Lam; **63:** Sergio TB/ Shutterstock; **64-65:** © Seth, photo Torresigner/Getty Images; **66:** The Mothership Connection by Zak Ové at the Shepherd. Courtesy of Zak Ové and Gallery 1957, photo PD Rearick; **67:** View from the Belt Detroit featuring murals by Rosson Crow and Jordan Nickel, photo by PD Rearick. Courtesy of Library Street Collective, Charles McGee Legacy Park at the Shepherd. Courtesy of the artist's estate and Library Street Collective, photo by Jason Keen; **68-69:** Jeff Kowalsky/Bloomberg via Getty Images; **70:** Aubrie Pick for Lonely Planet, Rachel Goad/Shutterstock; **71:** Courtesy of the Detroit Institute of Arts; **72:** JAUME PLENSA - The Crown Fountain, 2004, photo Laura Medina © Plensa Studio Barcelona © Jaume Plensa, VEGAP Madrid / IVARO Dublin, 2025; **73:** © Anish Kapoor. All Rights Reserved, DACS London / IVARO Dublin, 2025, photo Rolf 52/Shutterstock; **74:** Dining Room, Frederick C. Robie House (Frank Lloyd Wright, 1908-10), Chicago. Courtesy of Frank Lloyd Wright Trust, Chicago, photo James Caulfield; **75:** Chicago Avenue entrance, Frank Lloyd Wright Home and Studio (Frank Lloyd Wright, 1889-1909), Oak Park, Ill. Courtesy of Frank Lloyd Wright Trust, Chicago, photo James Caulfield; **76:** Elmgreen & Dragset, Prada Marfa, 2005, photo James Evans, 2020. Courtesy of Ballroom Marfa; **77:** Harmon Li for Lonely Planet; **78:** Meow Wolf's House of Eternal Return, images courtesy of Atlas Media; **79:** Danny Lehman/Getty Images, Art of Indigenous Fashion, image courtesy of IAIA Museum of Contemporary Native Arts (MoCNA), photo Nicole Lawe; **80:** Georgia O'Keeffe Museum, Interior. 2024. Santa Fe, New Mexico. © Georgia O'Keeffe Museum; **81:** Alfred Stieglitz. Georgia O'Keeffe, ca. 1930. Gelatin silver print, 3 9/16 x 4 1/2inches. Georgia O'Keeffe Museum. Museum Purchase. [2014.3.74]; **82:** Jenny Day, A Feast to Remember (Installation view), photo Byron Flesher | courtesy of form & concept, Justin Foulkes for Lonely Planet; **83:** Nancy Friedland Exhibition, photo Brad Trone; **84:** EQRoy/Shutterstock; **85:** de Young Museum, Diller Court, Andy Goldsworthy's "Drawn Stone", photo Courtesy of the Fine Arts Museums of San Francisco; **86:** Braunger/ullstein bild via Getty Images; **87:** MAESTRAPEACE Mural (1994 and 2000) by Juana Alicia Miranda Bergman, Edythe Boone, Susan Kelk Cervantes, Meera Desai, Yvonne Littleton, and Irene Perez, All Rights Reserved. maestrapeaceartworks.com. Photo Shelly Rivoli/Alamy; **88:** © Exploratorium, photo Ida Tietgen Hoeyrup, Stefano Politi Markovina/Shutterstock; **89:** Yhelfman/Shutterstock; **90:** Nik Wheeler/ Getty Images; **91:** Central Garden at the Getty Center designed by Robert Irwin, photo Cassia Davis © 2022 J. Paul Getty Trust; **92:** Benedek/iStock; **93:** (L to R) Justine Rafael, Madison Grepo, Mia Sempertegui, Leianna Weaver, and Sarah Marie Hernandez perform "My Junk" in Spring Awakening at East West Players, photo by Jenny Graham; **95:** The Broad Exterior, photo Mike Kelley. Courtesy of The Broad, Griffith Observatory, photo Ken Wolter/Shutterstock, Watts Towers by Simon Rodia, Simon Rodia State Historic Park, Los Angeles, 1921-1954, photo Walter Cicchetti/ Shutterstock, The Music Center's Walt Disney Concert Hall, photo Alisia Luther/ Shutterstock; **96:** Vicente Manuel Rosas Pereyna, "Vincitore", 2010, reed wood and paper (china paper), photo Sun_Shine/Shutterstock; **97:** Lonnie Kishiyama/Getty Images; **98:** Bettmann/Getty Images; **99:** Andrew Hasson/Getty Images; **100:** Dowraik/Shutterstock; **101:** Casa Gilardi by Luis Barragan, photo Yueqi Li/Alamy, Soumaya Museum, photo John Coletti/ Getty Images; **102:** Kelli Hayden/Shutterstock; **103:** Raul Luna/Shutterstock; **104:** Danny Lehman/Getty Images; **105:** Kristel Segeren/Shutterstock; **106:** Christian Vinces/ Shutterstock; **107:** Fotonio/Getty Images, Saiko3p/Shutterstock; **108:** Ben Pipe/AWL Images; **109:** Chef Virgilio Martínez Courtesy of Mater; **110:** Hélio Oiticica, Invention of Color, Penetrable Magic Square #5, De Luxe, Garden Center of Contemporary Art Inhotim, photo Ronaldo Almeida/Shutterstock; **111:** Olafur Eliasson, Viewing machine, 2003, Inhotim, CACI, Brumadinho, Brazil, 2008, photo Alex Robinson/AWL Images; **112-113:** Yayoi Kusama, Narcissus Garden, 1966/2009, stainless steel, photo Marcio.Duarte/Shutterstock; **114:** Ivo Antonie de Rooij/Shutterstock; **115:** James Yamada, Our Starry Night, 2008, Powder coated aluminum, metal detector, LED lights/Sur Creativa; **116-117:** Mario Irarrázabal, La Mano, 1982, photo Ksenia Ragozina/Shutterstock; **118:** Matt Munro for Lonely Planet; **119:** Lovelypeace/Shutterstock, Antonio Berni, The Great Temptation or The Great Illusion at MALBA, photo Santiago Ortí, courtesy of Malba; **120:** Diegograndi/Getty Images; **121:** Maurizio De Mattei/Shutterstock; **122:** Volanthevist/Getty Images; **123:** Mana Gallery photo © EISP Archives and Database; **124:** Yaopey Yong/Unsplash; **125:** © Estate of Karel Appel, Pictoright Amsterdam / IVARO Dublin, 2025, photo hedgehog111/Shutterstock; **126:** Leo Daphne/Alamy; **127:** teamLab, Universe of Water Particles on a Rock where People Gather, Flowers and People, Cannot be Controlled but Live Together – A Whole Year per Hour, Crows are Chased and the Chasing Crows are Destined to be Chased as well: Flying Beyond Borders, Interactive Digital Installation, Sound: Hideaki Takahashi © teamLab, courtesy Pace Gallery, Tokyo Kite Museum, photo Matt Munro for Lonely Planet; **128:** Portrait of Yayoi Kusama, photo by Yusuke Miyazaki © YAYOI KUSAMA; **129:** Yayoi Kusama, FLOWER OBSESSION (detail), 2017/2020, Installation view at Yayoi Kusama Museum, 2021, © YAYOI KUSAMA; **131:** 21_21 DESIGN SIGHT, photo Masaya Yoshimura, Center Atrium, photo courtesy: Mori Art Museum, Tokyo, © ASAKURA Museum of Sculpture; **132:** YAYOI KUSAMA, Pumpkin, 216 x 248.8 x 253.9cm, Mixed media, 2022, © YAYOI KUSAMA, photo by Rahil Chadha/Unsplash; **133:** Naoshima Port Terminal by artists KAZUYO SEJIMA + RYUE NISHIZAWA / SANAA - Artwork No. na09; **134:** Art House Project "Haisha" Shinro Ohtake" Dreaming Tongue/BOKKON-NOZOKI", photo OMOTE Nobutada; **135:** Art House Project "Go'o Shrine" Hiroshi Sugimoto "Appropriate Proportion", photo: Hiroshi Sugimoto; **136:** Nghia Khanh/Shutterstock; **137:** F16-ISO100/Shutterstock; **138:** MMCA Gwacheon © Park Jung Hoon; **139:** Reopening of The More, The Better, 2022, Photo Woo Jongduk, Commissioned by MMCA; **140:** Jinghui Cai/Lonely Planet; **141:** Cao Fei: Staging the Era, UCCA Center for Contemporary Art, 2021. Courtesy UCCA Center for Contemporary Art, Pictures from History/Bridgeman Images; **142-143:** Installation view of "Memory and Imagination: UCCA at Fifteen," UCCA Center for Contemporary Art, 2022. Photograph by Sun Shi, courtesy UCCA Center for Contemporary Art; **144:** 798 Art Zone, photo Simon Montgomery/robertharding/ Alamy; **145:** Zvonimir Atletic/Shutterstock; **146:** Museum of Nepali Art (MoNA); **147:** Bartosz Hadyniak/Getty Images; **148:** Kiran Manandhar, Beauties, 2013, Acrylic on Canvas, 159 X 96 cm, Museum of Nepali Art (MoNA); **149:** Studio Image: Kathmandu Art House; **150:** CRS PHOTO/Shutterstock; **151:** Savvapanf Photo/Shutterstock; **152:** Eddie Gerald/Alamy; **153:** PUNIT PARANJPE/AFP via Getty Images; **154:** BACC; **155:** Tuayai/iStock/Getty Images, Jon Arnold/AWL Images; **156-157:** Thailand Creative & Design Center (TCDC) photo, Creative Economy Agency (Public Organization); **158:** Mateescu Mircea Mugur/Shutterstock; **159:** Hafizzuddin/Shutterstock; **160:** Marc Quinn, "Planet", 2008, Gardens By The Bay, Singapore, 2013, photo DoublePHOTO studio/Shutterstock; **161:** Gigi/Unsplash; **162-163:** Wsboon images/Getty Images; **164:** StoriesFromAnywhere/Shutterstock; **165:** Keith Brian de Leon/ Unsplash; **166:** Anamejia18/Getty Images; **167:** Hemis/AWL Images; **168:** Courtesy of Einar Magnus Magnusson/Shutterstock; **169:** Christoph Wagner/Getty Images; **171:** Bragi Thor Josefsson/Getty Images; **172:** National Museum of Norway Collection, photo Iwan Baan; **173:** National Museum of Norway Collection, photo Iwan Baan, © Tracey Emin, All rights reserved, DACS London / IVARO Dublin, 2025, photo Xbrchx/Adobe Stock; **174:** CC BY-NC-SA 4.0 Munchmuseet / photo Ragnvald Væring; **175:** VISIT OSLO/photo Tord Baklund © Louise Bourgeois/BONO Ekebergparken, Louise Bourgeois 'The Couple' 2003, Ekeberg Park, © The Easton Foundation, ARS New York / IVARO Dublin, 2025; **176:** Chappe photo @ Tuomas Uusheimo; **177:** JKMM Amos Rex. Photo Mika Huisman, Amos Rex; **178:** Fiskars Village; **179:** Fiskars Village photo Risto Vauras; **180:** Jacob Dahlgren, Early One Morning, Eternity Sculpture, Helsinki, 2018, Size 1292 x 804 cm, Height: 379 cm, © Photo: Maija Toivanen / HAM Helsinki Art Museum; **181:** Kunsthalle Helsinki, photo Patrik Rastenberger, Ateneum Art Museum, photo: Finnish National Gallery, Aleks Talve; **182:** Anton Ivanov Photo, Adobe Stock; **183:** Claudio Divizia/Shutterstock; **184:** Hall window, the Mackintosh House © The

Hunterian, University of Glasgow; **185:** Studio-Drawing Room, the Mackintosh House © The Hunterian, University of Glasgow; **186:** Brian Scantlebury/Shutterstock; **187:** Minka Guides/ Shutterstock, Winston Tjia/Unsplash; **188:** Alex Segre/Shutterstock, 189: Marco Rubino/ Shutterstock, John Harper/Getty Images; **190:** Handel Hendrix House, photo Michael Bowles; **191:** James Bedford for Lonely Planet; **192:** Gareth Gardener © Sir John Soane's Museum, London, © The Trustees of the British Museum; **193:** Beyond The Streets, 2023, courtesy of Saatchi Gallery, London; **194:** STRAAT, photo Emzzi/Shutterstock, 195: Mark Read for Lonely Planet; **196:** Exhibition Gifts Unwrapped. Photo Tropenmuseum; **197:** Wereldmuseum Amsterdam building, photo Jordi Huisman; **198:** Excavation: St Kolumba 7th century | chapel Madonna in the Ruins 1949/1956 architect chapel Gottfried Boehm, architect superstructure Peter Zumthor, photo: Veit Landwehr © Kolumba Cologne 199: Photo Alexander Fischer, Cologne © Museum Ludwig, Cologne; **200:** Lady Pink painting the facade of the museum for the Exhibition "Love Letters to the City" at Urban Nation Museum in Berlin, September 2024, photo Nika Kramer/Stiftung Berliner Leben; **201:** Doin' it cool for the East Side, Jim Avignon, East Side Gallery 2018, Berlin Wall Foundation, photo Jascha Fibich, View Apart/Shutterstock; **202:** Katja Novitskova, Pattern of Activation, 2014, Photo: © Noshe; **203:** Martin Boyce, We Pass But Never Touch, 2003, Photo: © Noshe; **204:** Christian KERA Hinz - Pool Painting, Photo © Eugen Lebedew (Million Motions); **205:** Jonathan Stokes for Lonely Planet; **206:** C/O Berlin im Amerikahaus in Berlin Charlottenburg. © Foto: David von Becker; **206:** Archive Danubiana Meulensteen Art Museum photo Pavol Harum; **207:** Slovak National Gallery photo Martin Deko; **208-209:** Slovak National Gallery photo Matej Hakar; **210:** Andrei Rybachuk/ Shutterstock; **211:** TasfotoNL/Getty Images, Kunsthistorisches Museum Vienna, Picture Gallery © KHM Museumsverband; **212:** Leoks/Shutterstock; **213:** Kiev Victor/Shutterstock; **214:** Collection de l'Art Brut, Lausanne, photo Delphine Burtin; **215:** Westend61/Getty Images; **216:** Trabantos/ Shutterstock; **217:** Terrasse de la Brasserie de Montbenon, photo Colin Frei; **218:** Kim Rogerson/ Getty Images; **219:** Gimas/Shutterstock; **220:** Quentin Chevrier; **221:** POUSH, exhibition space at the Coupole, "Contact Zone" exhibition, 2023 © DR; **223:** PA_1213, Paris, 2016, Invader, © @Invader, ADAGP Paris / IVARO Dublin, 2025, © Culturespaces / C. de la Motte Rouge - ASTÉRIX ® OBELIX ® IDEFIX ® / © 2025 LES ÉDITIONS ALBERT RENE / GOSCINNY-UDERZO, Liberté, Egalité, Fraternité by Shepard Fairey/obeygiant.com, photo Quentin Touvard/Unsplash, Sokolovski/Shutterstock; **224:** Vicki Jauron, Babylon and Beyond Photography/Getty Images; **225:** Photo12/UIG/Getty Images; **226:** DEA / ALBERT CEOLAN/Getty Images; **227:** Photosmatic/Shutterstock; **228:** Hans Georg Eiben/AWL Images; **229:** Trabantos/Shutterstock; **230:** Matt Paco for Lonely Planet; **231:** Volkova Natalia/ Shutterstock, David Soanes Photography/Getty Images; **232:** Saiko3p/Shutterstock; **233:** Csp/ Shutterstock; **234:** Vlada Z/Shutterstock; **235:** Shaun Egan/Getty Images, Daniela Baumann/ Shutterstock; **236:** ArtesiaWells/iStock; **237:** Andrei Bortnikau/Shutterstock; **238-239:** © Estate of Juan Miro, ADAGP Paris / IVARO Dublin, 2025, photo Mark Green/Shutterstock; **240-241:** Giorgio Morara/Shutterstock; **241:** Photo: Marco Zorzanello, Courtesy Archivio Storico della Biennale di Venezia, ASAC; **242:** Paolo Veronese "Feast in the House of Levi", Gallerie dell'Accademia, Venice, photo Hercules Milas/Alamy; **243:** Museo Correr, photo Sylvain Sonnet/Getty Images; **244:** Jan Christopher Becke/AWL Images; **245:** Only Fabrizio/Shutterstock, Jupiter Images/Getty Images; **246:** Stockbym/Shutterstock; **247:** Essevu/Shutterstock; **248:** Richard A. McGuirk/Shutterstock, Roberto Serra - Iguana Press/Getty Images; **249:** Powerofforever/Getty Images; **250:** George Pachantouris/Getty Images; **251:** Paul Panayiotou/Getty Images; **252:** Courtesy of the Benaki Museum of Greek Culture; **253:** Peter Eastland/Alamy; **254:** Marcobrivio.photography/Shutterstock, Isidoros Andronos/Shutterstock; **255:** Courtesy of Dio Horia Gallery; **256:** Hercules Milas/Alamy; **257:** Klemen Misic/Adobe Stock; **258:** Cyprus Museum Nicosia, photo Sun_Shine/Shutterstock; **259:** Cyprus Museum, photo Jeremy Villasis. Philippines/Getty Images; **260:** Justin Foulkes for Lonely Planet; **261:** The Cafesjian Center for the Arts (Cafesjian Sculpture Garden), Sculpture: Fernando Botero (1932-2023), Colombia, Mujer Fumando un Cigarrillo (Woman Smoking a Cigarette), 1987, Bronze, dark brown patina The Gerard L. Cafesjian Collection, Kirill Skorobogatko/ Shutterstock; **262:** KrimKate/Shutterstock; **263:** Travel Photography/iStock; **264:** Grotto, 2017, Randy Polumbo, Mona/Jesse Hunniford, Image courtesy of the artist and Mona, Hobart, Tasmania, Australia; **265:** Wellington 'The Skin I Am In', Katherine Bertram, New Zealand; **266:** Chris Chen for Lonely Planet; **267:** EcoPrint/Shutterstock; **268:** Albacutya Silo Art - Victoria, Artist: Kitt Bennett, photo Kitt Bennett; **269:** GrainCorp Silos at Kaniva, Victoria by David Lee Pereira, photo Robert Wyatt/Alamy; **270:** Ymgerman/Shutterstock; **271:** Melbourne Mural by Steen Jones @steen_jones, Australia. 'Have Paint, Will Travel'. Photo Alexi Rosenfeld/Getty Images, Chris Putnam/Alamy; **272-273:** Heide Museum of Modern Art, 2024, photographs Clytie Meredith; **275:** Mona/Jesse Hunniford, Image courtesy of Mona, Hobart, Tasmania; **276:** Jack Driver/Shutterstock; **277:** Curves Ahead, Grace DuVal, United States; **279:** Visitors in Rongomaraeroa with a Host, 2019. Photo by Johnny Hendrikus. Te Papa; **281:** Len Lye Centre (Govett-Brewster Art Gallery), photo Wirestock/ iStock, QuiBee/Shutterstock; **282:** View of the Center: © ADCK – Tjibaou Cultural Center, photo M. Le Chélard; **283:** Lembi/Shutterstock; **284-285:** Totems in Jinu: © ADCK – Tjibaou Cultural Center, photo E. Dell'Erba; **286:** Eric Lafforgue/Getty Images; **287:** MJ Photography/Alamy; **288:** 4th floor, 101 Spring Street, Judd Foundation, New York. Photo Charlie Rubin © Judd Foundation. Frank Stella, Gur II, 1967 © Estate of Frank Stella, ARS New York / IVARO Dublin, 2025, The Diego Rivera and Frida Kahlo Home Studio, Mexico City, photo Brester Irina/Shutterstock; **289:** Merydolla/ Shutterstock; **290:** © Exploratorium, Meow Wolf, House of Eternal Return, photo Kate Russell; **291:** Peter Seaward for Lonely Planet; **292:** James Strachan/Getty Images, Yaopey Yong/Unsplash; **293:** Photo: Matteo De Mayda Courtesy Archivio Storico della Biennale di Venezia, ASAC; **300:** Paul Vowles/Shutterstock; **302-303:** © Fundació Junta Constructora del Temple Expiatori de la Sagrada Família; **Back Cover:** Isidoros Andronos/Shutterstock, Yaopey Yong/Unsplash, Guests visiting Rivera Court, Courtesy of the Detroit Institute of Arts.

Art Destinations
Project Editor Bridget Watson-Payne
Editors Karyn Noble, Polly Thomas
Designer Wynne Au-Yeung
Publishing Director Piers Pickard
Editorial Director Becca Hunt
Art Director Emily Dubin
Photo Editor Claire Guest
Indexer Connie Binder
Print Production Nigel Longuet

October 2025
Published by Lonely Planet Global Limited
CRN: 554153
ISBN: 978 18375 8518 2

10 9 8 7 6 5 4 3 2 1
Printed in Malaysia

STAY IN TOUCH
lonelyplanet.com/contact

Lonely Planet Office:
IRELAND
Digital Depot, Roe Lane (off Thomas St),
Digital Hub, Dublin 8, D08 TCV4, Ireland

Paper in this book is certified against the Forest Stewardship Council™ standards. FSC™ promotes environmentally responsible, socially beneficial and economically viable management of the world's forests.

p.300: *A flutter of fabric at Mexico's Museo Textil de Oaxaca, where displays showcase the region's woven art.* ***Previous spread:*** *The ornate ceiling in the nave of Antoni Gaudí's masterwork – the Sagrada Família in Barcelona, Spain.*